TITA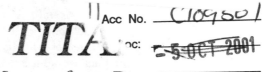

Voyage from Dru

Drumshee Timeline Ser
Book 6

Cora Harr.... ..... ht primary-school ... . in England for tw. .... .e years before moving ... all farm in Kilfenor.... Clare. The farm include. ... .on Age fort, with the r..mains of a small ... .sue .sid. it, and the mys'.rious atmosphere of .... ancient place gave Cora the idea for a .eries of ..storical novels tracing the survival of the ringfo. through the centuries. *Titanic — Voyage from Drumshee* follows *Nuala & her Secret Wolf*, *The Secret of the Seven Crosses*, *The Secret of Drumshee Castle*, *The Secret of 1798* and *The Famine Secret* in the Drumshee Timeline Series.

For Patrick Beggan, Patrick Lynch and Eoghan Lynch
of Inchovea School,
and with many thanks to Brian Doyle of Ennistymon Library
for his helpfulness in facilitating my use of the excellent resources
of Ennistymon Library.

OTHER TITLES BY CORA HARRISON

Nuala & her Secret Wolf
Drumshee Timeline Series Book 1

The Secret of the Seven Crosses
Drumshee Timeline Series Book 2

The Secret of Drumshee Castle
Drumshee Timeline Series Book 3

The Secret of 1798
Drumshee Timeline Series Book 4

The Famine Secret
Drumshee Timeline Series Book 5

TITANIC
Voyage from Drumshee

Drumshee Timeline Series
Book 6

Cora Harrison

Illustrated by Orla Roche

WOLFHOUND PRESS
& in the US and Canada
The Irish American Book Company

First published in 1998 by
Wolfhound Press Ltd
68 Mountjoy Square
Dublin 1, Ireland
Tel: (353-1) 874 0354
Fax: (353-1) 872 0207

Published in the US and Canada by
The Irish American Book Company
6309 Monarch Park Place
Niwot, Colorado 80503, USA

© 1998 Cora Harrison

The Arts Council
An Chomhairle Ealaíon

Wolfhound Press receives financial assistance from The Arts Council/An Chomhairle Ealaíon, Dublin, Ireland.

British Library Cataloguing in Publication Data
A catalogue record for this book is available from the British Library.

ISBN 0-86327-679-2

10 9 8 7 6 5 4 3

Wolfhound Press would like to thank Ed Coughlan, chairman of the Irish *Titanic* Historical Society, and Fr E.E. O'Donnell SJ, for helping to ensure that all information about the *Titanic* is as accurate as possible. Responsibility for any remaining errors rests with the author and publisher.

Cover illustration: Marie-Louise Fitzpatrick
Cover Design: Reprolink
Typesetting: Wolfhound Press
Printed and bound by The Guernsey Press Co., Guernsey, Channel Islands

CHAPTER ONE

*A*nd remember, Drumshee is your home now, and will be for as long as you like,' finished Uncle Mike.

'And we love having you. It's like having a big daughter as well as a little one,' put in Aunt Maggie.

'And it will be nice having young legs to fetch and carry for me,' laughed Granny.

Kitty muttered something and fled to her little loft bedroom. She couldn't choke back the tears any longer. She didn't know which was harder to bear: the sympathy of her uncle Mike and his wife Maggie, or the resolute cheerfulness of her grandmother, old Annie McMahon. Actually, Kitty thought, Granny's attitude is probably the worst. After all, I'm not feeling very cheerful ....

Kitty had lost her father, Mike's eldest brother Patrick, in a mining accident two years before. Her mother had worked as a seamstress to maintain Kitty and herself; but then, only two weeks before, she had died of consumption.

Granny could at least show that she's sorry, Kitty thought resentfully. Her tears began to flow again. She clenched her hands to stop the sobbing. Her throat was sore and her stomach hurt from crying. She undressed and got into bed. I'll stop crying tomorrow, she promised herself.

In the morning, when Kitty woke up, her throat was still sore and her eyes felt glued shut from all the tears she had shed. For a moment, she almost started to cry again; but then she sat up in bed, opened her eyes wide and listened.

Rain was pouring down, and the wind was howling — Kitty had never heard a wind like it. The huge old chestnut tree outside her window moaned and shrieked like a living thing as the wind rose to new heights. A broken branch struck the window, and there was a tinkle of glass.

Then it happened. There was a rumbling noise — a scream from downstairs, where Maggie was getting the breakfast — more rumbling — and then a crash.

Kitty jumped out of bed, hastily pulled on her dress over her petticoat, and stuffed her feet into her shoes. It was still as dark as night, and she could see nothing; but suddenly a flash of lightning, immediately followed by a crash of thunder, lit up the room. Kitty flung herself across the room and onto the ladder which led down to the kitchen. That one flash had shown her enough. The whole of the chimney wall had begun to crumble, and there was a large gaping hole in it.

In the darkness, Kitty almost crashed into Mike, who was on his way up to collect her. 'Good girl,' was all he said, but the steady note in his voice calmed her. She followed him down the ladder.

The kitchen was full of smoke, making Kitty cough. Mike caught her hand and pulled her outside. In the little cobbled yard she could make out the shapes of her grandmother, wound tightly in her old black shawl, and Maggie with the baby, Bridget, in her arms.

'Into the cow cabin with all of you,' said Mike. 'Best shelter there while I have a look at the chimney.'

The six cows were still in the cabin, tied to their stalls. They turned gentle, inquisitive eyes on the human intruders. Kitty looked at their astonished faces, and for the first time in days, she felt the beginnings of a smile tug at the corners of her mouth.

'They're trying to say that it's too early for milking,' said Mike cheerfully, patting the bony rump of the nearest cow. 'Here you are, Kitty, stroke old Daisy. She's the friendliest cow of the lot. She won't hurt you. She's tied up, anyway.'

Kitty shrank back nervously. Until a few days before, she had lived all her life in the city of Liverpool. She had never even seen a cow until she came to Drumshee.

She looked at the big, friendly animal and felt a little ashamed of herself. She had never been frightened of anything before; she had gone through the roughest streets of Liverpool, carrying sewing work for her mother, and had never even allowed herself to feel nervous.

Cautiously she stroked Daisy; then she sat down on the stool and leaned her cheek against the cow's hairy side. The cow smelt warm, and a little milky. It was a comforting smell. Kitty closed her eyes. Maggie and old Annie were talking eagerly; they were exclaiming over the damage the storm had caused, but Kitty didn't think they were too worried.

'That's the last of it,' said Annie thankfully. 'Listen; the wind is dying down. I never like a storm. Do you remember me telling you about the night of the Big Wind? I wasn't born then, but my Martin — God have mercy on him — he remembered it, and he told me about it so often that I feel as if I was there myself.'

'When did that happen, then?' Kitty could tell from the sound of Maggie's voice that she had heard the story many times. Probably she was straining her ears for sounds from the house, and at the same time trying to keep the seventy-year-old grandmother and the eighteen-month-old baby happy and calm in the cow cabin. Kitty began to feel a little ashamed of how useless she was being. She went to the door as her grandmother was saying, 'It was the sixth of January, 1837, and every house in the parish lost its thatch that night ....'

Kitty went outside. The rain had begun to ease off, and the black clouds were chasing one another across the sky. Even in the sheltered yard, she could feel the strength of the wind against the back of her head, blowing her thick black hair in front of her, almost blinding her. She went to the door of the little cottage and looked in.

'Uncle Mike?' she said hesitantly. There was no answer, so she moved cautiously into the kitchen. The smoke from the turf fire had begun to clear, and Kitty could see the kitchen in the dim light. Everything seemed as normal — the flagstoned floor, the settle, the dresser filled with old willow-pattern plates — except that an enormous stone had fallen down into the fireplace, bending the iron crane and knocking over the three-legged pot which normally stood on the embers.

'Uncle Mike,' Kitty said again. Mike appeared at the top of the stairs, his shock of red hair blazing in the gloom, a big grin on his freckled face.

'No harm done,' he said cheerfully. 'The other stones are quite firm. Come and see, though. There's something very strange up here.'

Kitty climbed up the ladder and into the loft. Mike had lit a candle, so although not much light came in through the west-facing window, she could see quite clearly what he was talking about.

'Look,' he said. 'Do you know, I've often wondered why the chimney had this little bit built onto it here. I thought it might be just a bit of a wall to shore up a weakness in the chimney, but look — it's like a tiny little room.'

Kitty looked, and gasped in excitement. You could hardly call it a room; it was about three feet wide and about four feet tall, barely big enough for a man to sit in. But it wasn't empty: inside it was a wooden chest, beautifully carved and carefully sealed with wax.

'That's some very expensive wood, that chest,' said Mike. 'I can't tell what it is, but smell it. It's got a kind of scent from it.'

'I wonder what's in it,' said Kitty, her voice trembling with excitement. 'Do you know how old it is?'

Mike shrugged his shoulders. 'Well, I've never heard about a chest,' he said, 'and my father was born here in this cottage in the year 1833, and I'm pretty sure he didn't know about it either.'

'Let's open the chest,' said Kitty eagerly. 'There might be treasure in it!'

Mike laughed. 'Well, treasure or no treasure, it will have to wait until after breakfast. I can hear young Bridget beginning to yell. She'll want her porridge and there'll be no peace until she gets it. Come on down and help me with the fire.'

Kitty bounded happily down the ladder. Quite suddenly, her depression seemed to have lifted.

Mike rolled the huge boulder outdoors, and Kitty set to work coaxing the fire with small pieces of dry turf, while Maggie scraped as much porridge as she could out of the upturned pot. It was the first time Kitty had ever lit a fire with turf, and she found that it was quite different from coal. She liked the smell of it, though, and she liked the clean smell of the air sweeping in through the open doors. She went to the door, sniffed, and then licked her lips curiously. They tasted of salt.

'That's a wind straight off the Atlantic Ocean,' said her grandmother, watching her with a smile. 'There's great health in that wind.'

I wonder, Kitty thought: if we'd come over here after Daddy died, instead of staying in Liverpool, would Mammy have lived? She quickly pushed the thought to the back of her mind. She would not think about her mother. She would just think about what might be in that old chest.

'We found a chest upstairs, Granny — me and Uncle Mike,' she said hurriedly, sitting down beside her grandmother. 'Do you know anything about it?'

'You know that bulge by the chimney wall, up in the loft?' Mike put in. 'Well, there was something like a little cupboard inside that wall, and in it was this chest, all sealed up with wax. Did you know it was there, Mother?'

'No, I didn't,' said old Annie, turning the matter over in her mind. 'I never heard of anything of the sort. I don't think Martin — God have mercy on him — knew about it either. If he'd known, and there had been anything in it worth selling, we'd have sold it long ago. We had some hard times, when the potato

failed again and again and we had five boys to feed
.... I wonder what could be in the chest?'

'Well, we'll all go and have a look after breakfast,'
said Maggie, smiling at Kitty. 'Hold Bridget for me,
pet, while I make a sup of tea for us all. Thank God I
made the bread before that happened. There's only
enough porridge for Bridget, but the rest of us can
have a bit of griddle bread and some good strong tea.'

Kitty chewed on the bread happily. She found that
she was very hungry. She had eaten hardly anything
for the last few days. The bread had a lovely nutty
taste; it had a flavour of something strange — the
turf smoke, perhaps. Whatever it was, Kitty was so
hungry that she ate three slices of the bread, thickly
smeared with Maggie's creamy butter.

After breakfast, all the family, including Bridget,
climbed up the ladder into the little loft bedroom.
Mike had roughly mended the hole in the chimney
with a few stones, but smoke welled out through the
gaps, making their eyes water.

'Wait a minute,' said Mike. 'I'll just run down and
get a bucket of wet mud, and I'll plaster around the
stones. Open the window, Kitty, and let a bit of air
into the place.'

In a few minutes, Mike was back, running lightly
up the steps with a bucket of wet mud and a trowel.
Quickly he smeared mud over the cracks; then,
picking up the wooden chest as effortlessly as if it
had been a cushion, he carried it over to the window.
Kitty knelt on the floor beside it.

'It's been well sealed,' said Mike, getting out his
knife. 'We'll keep this wax — it's real beeswax. Give
me a piece of cloth, Kitty, and I'll scrape it into that. It

will do for a candle afterwards.'

Kitty found a pocket handkerchief. It gave her a pang to look at it; her mother had made it. Kitty looked at the painstaking, slightly uneven stitches around the edge. Her mother had not been a good seamstress; Kitty herself was far better, and she knew that, without her efforts, the two of them might have starved.

Blinking her tears away, Kitty laid the handkerchief on the floor and forced herself to stare resolutely at the chest. Whatever comes out of it, she vowed, I will think of that and of nothing else for the rest of the day. I can't spend the rest of my life crying.

Mike dug deep with his knife, carefully peeling the wax away. 'I wouldn't be surprised if it were hundreds of years old,' he said. 'Look at how brown the wax is.'

All around the lid he went, scoring the wax and peeling it off, and everyone watched. Even little Bridget seemed to catch some of the excitement; she giggled to herself, waving her hands in the air.

At last the lid was free, and Mike opened the chest.

Kitty gave a gasp, and then a little sigh of ecstasy. There, lying in the old chest, was the most beautiful dress she had ever seen. It had a wide skirt of deep rose-pink velvet, over a cream silk underdress embroidered with pale pink roses.

'May I pick it up?' she asked excitedly.

'Do, pet,' said her grandmother. 'Hold it up and let us see what it would look like on you.'

Kitty picked up the lovely dress and held it against her body for a moment, before putting it carefully on the bed.

Underneath the first dress there was another one, made of purple velvet with a pale mauve underskirt; under that was a green silk, and then a royal-blue satin; and, last of all, there was a white brocade trimmed with crimson. Here and there the dresses had frayed, and some of the delicate lace had crumbled away, but on the whole they were in wonderful condition.

'I suppose it was being built into the chimney that kept them good,' said Maggie, holding little Bridget's hands away from the exquisite dresses. 'It's a pity some of them are torn. They should be mended, really, but I'm not much good at that sort of thing.'

Kitty looked up with shining eyes. 'Could I do it?' she asked eagerly. 'I'm very good at sewing, and I'd love to do it.'

She was conscious of Mike and Maggie exchanging glances, above her head, and smiling. They're happy I'm feeling so much better, she thought.

Suddenly Kitty felt a flood of contentment. Drumshee was becoming her home.

CHAPTER TWO

$\mathcal{F}$or the next week, the weather was wet and windy, but Kitty did not care. Day after day, she sat at the table by the window and mended the lovely dresses. By the end of the week, they were almost as good as new.

The sun shone briefly that day, and the wind dropped to a light breeze. Kitty hung each dress on a hanger and tied them securely to the washing-line to air them. It was a lovely sight: each of the dresses looked like a beautiful lady, dancing and twisting and turning in the wind. Maggie and old Annie came out to look, and baby Bridget screamed with delight.

When Kitty brought the dresses back in, and folded them carefully before replacing them in the chest, she could see that Maggie was thinking hard.

'I've been wondering if we could sell those dresses to Mrs Neylon, the dressmaker in Corofin,' Maggie said. 'She makes clothes for all the fine ladies around here. There are a lot of big houses around Lake Inchiquin, and she gets plenty of work from them. She could remake some of these in today's fashions, or else she could use them for those fancy-dress balls — masques, they call them — where all the fine ladies and gentlemen dress up in costumes from long ago.'

Kitty opened her mouth to protest, but then shut it again. She did not like the thought of the clothes being sold, but it was not for her to say. They weren't her clothes. It was very kind of Mike and Maggie to take in a penniless orphan, and no doubt it was costing them money to keep and feed her.

Maggie, however, saw her expression and gave her a sympathetic look.

'I know it would be nice to keep them,' she said, 'but just think — neither you nor I will ever be able to wear something like that, and your grandmother's dancing days are over. I've got an idea, though, that I think you might like. You're a great girl at the sewing, and I think it would be a nice idea to apprentice you to Mrs Neylon. She might be willing to take the dresses instead of a fee, and she could teach you everything she knows. Then you'd always be able to earn your living.'

'I'd love that,' said Kitty shyly. 'Thank you very much.' She said it awkwardly, but she could see that Maggie and Mike were smiling and that they knew she was pleased.

'And I've got an old bicycle out there that I don't use too often,' Maggie went on. 'You'll be able to cycle in and out of Corofin every day, so you'll still be able to live at home.'

It was the word 'home' that did it. For the first time in a week, Kitty began to cry. But, on the whole, they were happy tears. It was lovely to have a new home, and to have people caring for her and thinking about her future. For years, she had been the one taking responsibility for a sick mother, worrying about where the next meal was going to come from .... Now Maggie and Mike were petting her and looking after her, as though she were a child again.

'She takes after Martin's sister Deirdre,' said Annie.

'Martin said she was a wonder at sewing. She made lace. She made a lot of money, too. Many's the time she helped us out, even after she had her own family. She married a man called Mantel, over in London. She's dead now, and I suppose he is too.'

Kitty listened with interest, her tears drying on her face. Perhaps it was true; perhaps that was where she had got her ability to sew. Perhaps she, too, could make a lot of money ....

She picked up little Bridget and kissed the baby's soft coppery curls.

'Let's do a dance, Bridget,' she said.

'Want pwetty dwess,' said Bridget.

'When you're a big girl,' promised Kitty. 'Kitty will make you a pretty dress when you're a big girl.'

The next morning, Mike harnessed the Connemara pony to the ancient cart and hoisted the chest onto the back of it. Maggie climbed up beside him, and Kitty ran all the way down the avenue to open the gate for them. She was glad to run; she was feeling so excited that she couldn't stay still.

To be apprenticed to a dressmaker! That had always been her mother's dream for her. Every time Kitty had done a fine piece of sewing, her mother had sighed and said, 'If only we could get you apprenticed to a dressmaker. I've got nothing left to teach you.'

The cart rattled and bumped over the stony lanes. In less than an hour, they were clattering over the bridge and down the main street of the quiet little village of Corofin.

'Stop right outside the dressmaker's, Mike,' said Maggie. 'It's starting to rain, and we don't want any water to get on those lovely dresses.'

Mike, however, was not able to stop outside the dressmaker's shop; the place was already taken by a very smart motor car. Kitty had seen cars in Liverpool, but Mike was open-mouthed with admiration.

'It must be Lady Victoria,' whispered Maggie. 'That's Lady Victoria Fitzgerald, the daughter of old Lady Fitzgerald,' she added, to Kitty. 'We'd better not go in, Mike; we'll come back a bit later. Lady Victoria must be talking to Mrs Neylon.'

'Oh, bother that,' said Mike, impatiently. 'What makes Lady Victoria so much better than us, anyway? You march straight in there. Who knows, she might take a fancy to some of those dresses. It's a great opportunity.'

Kitty giggled. I do like Uncle Mike, she thought. He's a lot younger than Daddy; he must be less than ten years older than I am. He's more like a big brother than an uncle.

Inside the shop, the dressmaker was curtsying and saying, 'Yes, my lady; certainly, my lady.' Lady Victoria, a tall woman with a hooked nose and a stylish walking suit, was preparing to go. When she saw the chest, however, she stopped and looked at it inquisitively.

'What beautiful workmanship,' she said. She sniffed the chest, in a well-bred way, and ran her finger over its carved surface. 'That's sandalwood, is it not? What have you got in there?'

Maggie still seemed overawed by Lady Victoria, so Kitty curtseyed, in imitation of the dressmaker. 'We've got some beautiful dresses, my lady,' she said. 'Would you like to see them? They're made of the loveliest materials.'

Lady Victoria smiled. 'Well, open the chest, my man,' she commanded.

Mike looked annoyed, but he opened the chest. Lady Victoria's eyes widened.

'Why, they are beautiful,' she said, taking out the dresses one by one and handing them carefully to the dressmaker. 'Where on earth did you get them? Do you realise that these dresses must be about three hundred years old?'

Kitty and Maggie gasped in astonishment.

'Three hundred years!' said Maggie. 'How on earth did they last that length of time?'

'It is extraordinary,' said Lady Victoria, picking up the dress of purple silk and feeling it carefully. 'Where did you find them?' she repeated.

'Well, it was the wind — I mean, a stone fell out of the chimney,' explained Kitty, the words tumbling over one another with excitement. 'And they were there — in a sort of little room, just next to the chimney.'

'They were walled in,' put in Mike. 'They were in that chest, and the chest was sealed with wax. And of course, we always keep a fire going, summer and winter, so they stayed dry; and the wax stopped any insects, moths and such like, getting into them.'

'Look at this one,' said Kitty eagerly, forgetting in her excitement that she was talking to a great lady. 'The one with the pink velvet overskirt. It's my favourite. Look at the way the rosebuds on the underdress match the colour of the overskirt.'

'These should be in a museum,' said Lady Victoria. 'I'm sure the Victoria and Albert Museum in London would be most interested. Could I buy them from you? I will give you twenty pounds for them.'

'Twenty pounds!' gasped Kitty. She looked eagerly at Maggie and Mike. Surely that would be more than enough to pay her apprenticeship fee and have some money left over for the family! Mike was looking quite stunned.

Lady Victoria went on examining the dresses in an unconcerned way.

'I see there has been some mending done,' she said.

Kitty's heart seemed to stop suddenly. Perhaps Lady Victoria would not want the dresses after all ....

Lady Victoria, however, was showing the mended piece to Mrs Neylon. 'Exquisite work,' she murmured.

'Kitty did that,' said Maggie proudly.

Kitty's heart began to beat again, and the colour rose to her cheeks.

'Really!' said Lady Victoria, looking at her with interest. 'You sew very well, my dear. You are not from here, are you? Are you a relation of these people?'

'Kitty is living with us,' said Maggie. 'Her home is with us at Drumshee. She's our niece.'

'And your parents?'

'My father and mother are dead,' said Kitty quietly.

Lady Victoria looked at her thoughtfully, and then turned back to Maggie and Mike. 'Well, what do you say? Will you accept twenty pounds?'

Mike nodded. 'That seems a fair offer,' he said, in such an offhand way that Kitty could see Maggie was quite embarrassed. Lady Victoria, however, did not seem to notice. She appeared to be thinking hard.

'Good,' she said absent-mindedly. 'Could you drive the chest over to the house? I will meet you there. You go first, so that my motor car will not frighten your pony.'

She turned to Kitty. 'Would you like to ride in my motor car?' she asked.

'Oh, I'd love to,' said Kitty excitedly, only just remembering in time to add, 'your ladyship.'

The chauffeur drove so smoothly that Kitty hardly noticed that they were moving. Lady Victoria kept her busy answering questions about her schooling, and what she had done in England, and what she wanted to do in the future; Kitty was quite surprised when she realised that they had stopped in front of a handsome big house facing the river.

The chauffeur jumped out and opened the door of the car. Lady Victoria got out gracefully and Kitty hurriedly squeezed out after her, feeling rather embarrassed that the magnificent-looking chauffeur had to wait for her.

'Come into the house,' said Lady Victoria to Maggie and Mike, who were waiting by the pony's head. 'And you come too, Kitty. There is something I want to ask you.'

Kitty followed Maggie and Mike into Corofin House. The parlour was the most luxurious room she had ever seen or imagined. The walls were covered with ivory-coloured paper embossed with red and gold, and the curtains and carpet and the big soft armchairs were of deep red velvet. Kitty and Maggie sat side by side on a splendid sofa; Mike stood by the window, looking out at the river.

'You see,' Lady Victoria continued, 'next week I am going to America. I am taking my little niece and nephew with me; we are going to stay with the children's uncle, in New York, for six months. I want to take the children on a holiday; they have recently lost their parents, and I think it would be a good distraction for them. I need a girl to look after the children on the journey and during the holiday, and I would like to have someone who can keep their clothes in order and do some mending for me as well. I think Kitty would be ideal. She is young and lively and can sew beautifully. It would be a great experience for her, and she would be back in six months. What do you think?'

Maggie and Mike looked at each other in amazement, and then at Kitty. She sat very still and thought hard. One part of her felt quite panicky, but another part was wildly excited. To see America, to go across the ocean in a big ship ... she would always be sorry if she missed the opportunity.

Kitty looked at Maggie. 'I think I'd like to go, if you agree,' she said. 'I'll miss Drumshee and all of you, but six months isn't long, and I'd love to see America.'

'And what do you say?' enquired Lady Victoria, looking from Maggie to Mike.

'What I say,' said Mike steadily, 'is that Kitty is like our own daughter and we'd be sad to see her go, but she's fourteen years old and it's her decision. If she wants to go, then she can go with our blessing.'

'Good. That's settled, then,' said Lady Victoria, getting to her feet. 'Here is the money for the dresses. I shall return the chest to you, and perhaps one of the dresses, if I find that the Victoria and Albert Museum does not want them all.'

Maggie and Kitty curtseyed, and Mike gave a slight bow. They turned to go, but Lady Victoria stopped them; she went to a beautifully carved writing-desk by the window, opened a drawer and took out a leaflet.

'Here you are,' she said to Kitty. 'This will tell you all about the ship which will take us to America. It is the biggest ship in the world, and it is quite unsinkable. It is called the *Titanic*.'

CHAPTER THREE

The journey home was a joyful one. Maggie kept turning the twenty-pound note in her hands and planning the clothes that she would buy for Kitty.

'And for Bridget, and for yourself and Granny,' Kitty insisted.

'And what about for your poor Uncle Mike?' asked Mike.

'You don't deserve anything. You weren't polite enough,' said Maggie, pretending to be cross.

'All right, then. I'll go off on the *Titanic* too, if I'm not appreciated around here,' said Mike, dropping his voice to a nasal whine.

Kitty laughed. She could not remember when she had last felt as happy and lively as this. Her mother had been sick for such a long time that Kitty felt as if everything before her father's death and her mother's illness was only a distant dream.

'Mind you,' added Mike, in his normal voice, 'I'd give anything to go on the *Titanic*. It would be something you'd remember for the rest of your life. I must have a proper read of that leaflet when we get home, Kitty.'

When they got home, however, all the laughter and the good humour died down. At first, old Annie refused to believe that Kitty was going to America in a week's time; then she got angry and said that she would not allow her to go. Finally she sat down on the old settle beside the fireplace and began to cry, rocking herself to and fro in her distress.

'She'll drown, that's what will happen to her. That's what happened to all the ones who had to leave Ireland and go to America. They drowned, nearly all of them drowned. Coffin ships, they called them ....'

'But, Mother,' said Mike patiently, sitting down beside her, 'the ships are different nowadays. Those old ships were too small, and they had too many people on them. But Kitty will be going in the lap of luxury. Look at the picture of the ship. It's all shiny new. Lady Victoria says it's the biggest ship in the world and it's unsinkable.'

'She's not to go, I tell you!' cried old Annie, lifting her head. 'She'll drown, or something terrible will happen. You think you know everything, but you don't. You don't listen to me any more.'

Kitty bit her lip. She hated her grandmother to be upset, but she was not afraid. Still, though, she did not want to hear talk like that.

Mike looked around him in despair. Maggie caught his eye, frowned, and jerked her head towards the door. Mike got to his feet, patting his mother awkwardly on the arm, and moved away.

'I'll just get you a sup of tea, Mother, and then you'll feel better,' said Maggie, moving the arm of the crane over the fire and hanging the blackened kettle from the lowest hook. 'Kitty, you go and help Mike to put in the ducks, and then we'll all have some tea. God be praised, Bridget is still asleep.'

I wish Bridget was here, thought Kitty. It was hard to be sad when Bridget was around, with her copper curls and her ravishing smiles and her continual demands for attention.

'Why is Granny so upset?' Kitty asked Mike, as she helped him fill the ducks' dishes with clean water and oats.

'Well, at the time of the Famine, about sixty years ago, there were a lot of people died on those ships, that's true,' said Mike briefly. 'But, on the other hand,' he added, 'there were a lot of people who didn't die, and who went on to make a great success of life in America. You see them coming over here with gold watches, and gold stopping in their teeth, and expensive clothes on their backs.'

'I'd like to go,' said Kitty thoughtfully. 'I suppose Granny thinks it's taking a chance.'

'Life's a chance, you know,' said Mike. 'You could go down to the River Fergus, at the bottom of the hill, and you could trip and hit your head on a stone and drown in a couple of feet of water. No one can ever be sure of being safe. So take your chance. It's a great opportunity for you, and if you want to go — well, you just go. Patrick — your father — would want it for you. He was as brave as a lion. He was the most adventurous of the lot of us. When he was only ten years old he climbed to the top of Inchovea Castle, up the ruined walls, just holding on to the ivy. I'll show you the place in a minute, when we get the ducks in. He would do anything, would Patrick. He was a character. And you're the living image of him — the big blue eyes and the black hair.'

Kitty smiled. She liked to hear about her father. I'll be a character too, she thought.

'I'm like that, too,' she said aloud. 'I'm never afraid of anything.'

'Well, you stand over there, Miss Fearless Kitty

McMahon, and I'll drive the ducks down, and with a bit of good luck we'll get them in the duck-house quickly. And if I say any words that I shouldn't, just you close your ears to them.'

When the ducks were safely locked in, they strolled down the lane and Mike showed Kitty Inchovea Castle, an ivy-covered ruin beside a tumbling waterfall.

'Come back, now,' he said after a moment. 'I want to show you something else before it gets dark.'

They walked down the little lane, and Mike pointed out two rings of stones on the hillside opposite.

'There was a man came here once,' he said. 'I think he was what's called an archaeologist. He came to look at our old *cathair* up there — your father told you about the fort?'

'I think so,' said Kitty uncertainly. She did not like to admit that she could remember very little about her father. It was almost as if, after his death, she had blotted him out of her memory.

'Well, anyway, that archaeologist said those were holding rings for cattle, and he thought they were at least a couple of thousand years old. And so is the fort, or even older. Let's go up and see it.'

The fort was a circular enclosure, about a hundred yards across, completely surrounded by a stone wall and by blackthorn bushes. In the middle of the field, Mike stopped.

'This secret that I'm going to show you is something that only our family knows about. You must promise not to tell anyone outside the family about it,' he said.

'I promise,' said Kitty, beginning to feel excited.

Mike bent down and, with his large muscular

hands, tore up a few loose sods of grass. Underneath them was a heavy flagstone. Mike put the tips of his fingers under the edge of it and tumbled it over, and Kitty saw a flight of stone steps leading down into the earth.

'It's called a souterrain,' Mike explained. 'That means "underground". It's an underground room. Come down and see.'

There wasn't much light, but Mike went first and Kitty groped her way behind. 'One more step and you're at the bottom,' came Mike's voice. 'Wait a minute until I light the lantern. There — now you can see the place properly.'

Kitty looked around the little room. Three sides were made of squared-off blocks of limestone, but the fourth wall was made of heavy, irregular green-stone boulders. On the floor stood six huge pots. At one end of the room was a small shelf; Mike reached up to it and took down a small, heavy box. It was a strange box, dull grey in colour, with a pattern of interlacing shapes on the lid.

'Hold the lantern for me while I open it,' commanded Mike, and Kitty took the lantern, peering curiously into the box. Inside it was an envelope. Mike opened it.

To Kitty's astonishment, he took out a gold necklace and held it up before her.

Kitty gasped. It was the most beautiful thing she had ever seen. It was made of two delicate ribbons of gold, twisted together; on one end was a small loop, on the other an elaborately ornamented hook.

'Is it really gold?' she asked in awe.

Mike nodded. 'Yes,' he said. 'It's really gold.'

He undid the necklace and clasped it around Kitty's neck.

'It's for you,' he said.

'For me?' said Kitty, almost horrified. 'It can't be!'

'Yes, it is. It was found by my Aunt Fiona, your great-aunt, in this very souterrain. She gave it to my father, Martin, because he was the only one of the family to stay at home. He always said it would go to his eldest daughter, but of course he only had five boys. And then when you were born — the eldest daughter of his eldest son — he said that it would be for you, when you came over to Drumshee. Even when he was dying, he said to me, "Remember: the necklace for Patrick's girl." I think my mother was a bit annoyed that it didn't go to her; but, sure, what would she be doing with a gold necklace around the farm? You can have it to wear in America. Maggie reminded me of it this morning.'

Kitty could say nothing. She was blazing with excitement. What a pity I couldn't have kept one of the dresses we found in the loft! she thought. With a beautiful dress and a gold necklace, I'd be the equal of any grand lady in the land.

'Come inside and show it to your Granny,' said Mike. 'Perhaps that will cheer her up. Don't take too much notice of her. She's old and a bit crotchety. She was looking forward so much to you coming that she's disappointed that you're off again — but, sure, we'll hardly notice the time until you're back with us, please God.'

However, when Kitty went back indoors, her grandmother was still not too pleased with her.

'What are you wearing that necklace for?' she grumbled. 'You'll lose it, or you'll break it. That necklace is valuable.'

'Uncle Mike says I can take it with me to America,' said Kitty proudly. 'I might be able to wear it to a party or a dance there.'

'No! No, you can't!' shrieked her grandmother, leaping up from the settle and waving her stick in the air. 'You can't take that necklace out of here. The necklace must never leave Drumshee, or bad luck will follow!'

CHAPTER FOUR

*T*he next morning, a smart pony and trap struggled up the steep avenue to Drumshee and drew up in front of the little cottage. A fashionably dressed footman jumped out and looked around the farmyard with a certain amount of disdain. Hens everywhere, sharply pouncing on insects among the cobbles; ducks on their daily parade to the rich grass of the House Meadow; cows wandering out of the cow cabin, leaving the inevitable steaming piles of droppings behind them .... This is not the sort of thing that I am used to, his expression said.

'Yes?' said Mike impatiently. 'What are you looking for?'

The footman touched his hat, the gesture only just hiding his contempt.

'Message for Kitty McMahon,' he said briefly. 'Her ladyship's nephew and niece have just arrived. Her ladyship would like Kitty to spend a few hours with them at the house, so that the children can get to know her and she can be fitted for her uniforms.'

'When do you want her to go?' asked Mike.

'If she could go now, it would be convenient,' said the footman smoothly. 'She can come with me, and I'll bring her back here in a few hours' time.'

'Well, Kitty,' said Mike loudly, 'what do you think? Would it be convenient for you?'

Kitty suppressed a giggle with difficulty.

'I think I will go, Uncle Mike,' she said with dignity.

31

'It will be convenient to have the uniforms fitted now, so there will be plenty of time for any alterations, and I would like to meet the children.'

Privately, she thought that she would like to get away from her grandmother's moaning and sighing for a while. The morning had not been pleasant — nothing but warnings and prophecies and head-shakings. Quickly Kitty whispered the news to Maggie, kissed her grandmother, leaving the explanations to Maggie, and was on the trap in less than five minutes.

'Drive on,' she said cheekily to the footman, and heard Mike's laugh ring in her ears.

'I'm a free man,' he had said to her the night before. 'I own this farm, all twenty acres. My father was a tenant, and all his life he had to bow and scrape to the landlord and to the landlord's agent; but now it's 1912 and we don't need to do that any longer. Please God, one of these days Ireland might be a free country.'

When the trap drove up to Corofin House, the two children were waiting outside, an enormous dog standing beside them. They were prettily dressed — the little boy in an immaculately white sailor suit, with a whistle around his neck, and the little girl in a candy-striped pink dress, with a straw hat trimmed with rosebuds. The boy's a lovely-looking little fellow, thought Kitty, as she jumped out of the trap and went to meet them. He came up to her with his hand outstretched and a smile on his little face. He was about seven, and as pretty as a picture, with deep blue eyes and a head of blond curls.

'My name is Robert, and the dog is Toby. He's a Great Dane,' he said. 'Are you Kitty?'

'Yes, I am,' said Kitty. She wondered whether she should kiss him, but she decided just to shake hands, which Robert did with great self-possession.

'And what's your name?' she asked, turning to the little girl.

'Tabitha,' said the girl ungraciously, and turned her back. She was a year or two older than her brother, and very different from him in appearance: he was so blond, and she was very dark, with olive skin and dark brown eyes and hair.

'Are you looking forward to going to America?' asked Kitty.

'I'm looking forward to seeing the *Titanic*,' said Robert. 'It's got its own swimming pool, and eight decks. Do you know, it's so big that it's nearly half a mile long if you walk around the deck!'

'It's not half a mile long, then, stupid,' snapped Tabitha. 'It's not even a quarter of a mile.'

'Tabitha!' Lady Victoria had appeared on the steps. 'Don't speak so rudely to your brother. That child is so difficult,' she added, turning to Kitty. 'I simply don't know what to do with her. The boy is a little darling, but the girl is so rough. Plain-looking child, too, unfortunately.'

Tabitha heard that, thought Kitty. I'm sure she heard it. She tried to think of something to say, some way to praise Tabitha, but she couldn't find the right words. Tabitha turned and walked away.

'Be very firm with her,' said Lady Victoria. 'You will be in charge of them, so they both must obey you. I don't think you'll have much trouble with Master Robert, but Miss Tabitha will be more difficult.'

So I'm supposed to call them 'Miss' and 'Master',

thought Kitty. Uncle Mike wouldn't think much of that, but I don't care. I have a chance to see America, and I'll make the most of it. I wonder if I'll have to call the dog 'Master Toby'.

'Come inside, my dear,' said Lady Victoria. 'I'll hand you over to Mrs Davoren, the housekeeper, and she will show you your uniform. Then you can take Miss Tabitha and Master Robert for a walk beside the river. That will pass the morning nicely. In the afternoon I shall take them to see their grandfather, their poor mother's father.'

Kitty thought the uniform was lovely. It was a pretty blue dress, almost exactly Kitty's size.

'I'll be able to alter that in no time,' she told the housekeeper, looking at herself in the long mirror. 'I'll just shorten it a bit and take it in at the waist.'

'It goes well with your blue eyes,' said Mrs Davoren, who was a friendly, motherly woman. 'Now, let's just brush your hair. Let me see — I think I have an Alice band here in the drawer. Put that on before you put on the cap, to keep your hair back. God bless you, you have a lovely head of hair. Pity it doesn't curl, but it feels like silk and it has a lovely shine on it. Put the cap on, now, and here's the little apron.'

The cap and the apron were made of snow-white cotton trimmed with lace. Kitty looked in the mirror and smiled at herself. She disagreed with the housekeeper: she liked her straight black hair. She thought that it made her look more unusual, and it set off the lacy cap to perfection. She tried to imagine what she would have looked like in the pink velvet dress. If only her grandmother's cottage had a mirror in it!

Now she would never know.

'Mrs Davoren, when is Lady Victoria going to take those dresses that I found to London?' she asked.

'They're going by post,' said Mrs Davoren, taking several pairs of long black stockings out of a drawer. 'I don't think she's going to send them all, though. One of them has a stain on it.'

I wonder which one that is, thought Kitty. She hadn't noticed a stain, but then, the light in the little cottage had not been very good during that wet week when she had been mending the dresses. She had just opened her mouth to ask when suddenly, from outside the window, there came the sound of angry shouting, a child's high-pitched scream, and then Lady Victoria's commanding voice.

'Tabitha, you bad child, let go of your brother instantly!'

'You'd better get changed and go down quickly,' said Mrs Davoren. 'Lady Victoria is at her wits' end with those children. Of course, she never had any of her own, and she's a bit old for them, to tell the truth.'

'Is she married?' asked Kitty, quickly taking off the blue dress and pulling on her own clothes.

'Lady Victoria? No, she never married. Too fussy by half. She won't marry now, I should think; she must be forty years old. Still, it's just as well, I suppose. Lady Fitzgerald — that's Lady Victoria's mother — is a widow, and she's bedridden. It's a good job Lady Victoria is here to keep her company .... There, you're fine now. Just go down and see if you can help.'

When Kitty reached the terrace, Robert, still wailing, was sitting on his aunt's knee, his small round chin tilted to the sky, displaying an angry red weal around his neck. Tabitha was huddled in a corner, sobbing bitterly.

'Look at what that bad girl did to her little brother,' said Lady Victoria in an outraged tone.

Kitty knelt down and touched Robert's neck carefully. The skin was not broken, but it looked sore. He's more frightened than hurt, she thought.

'Where's Toby gone, then?' she said cheerfully.

Robert sat up and looked at her in surprise.

'Tabitha pulled me by the neck with my whistle,' he said severely.

'She could have strangled him,' said Lady Victoria.

Tears welled up in Robert's eyes again, and the corners of his mouth turned down.

'Blow your whistle,' said Kitty quickly. 'Blow your whistle and make Toby come. He'll look after you.'

The corners of Robert's mouth began to turn up again. He sat up a little straighter and blew an ear-piercing blast on the whistle that hung around the neck of his sailor suit. There was a clicking of claws on the gravel and Toby padded around the corner, looking big enough to look after an army of little boys.

'There you are,' said Kitty. 'You take him for a walk. March up and down the terrace just like a soldier.'

'I'm not a soldier, I'm a sailor,' said Robert, but he slid off his aunt's knee and went off, resting his little hand on Toby's neck.

'Do you think he will be all right?' asked Lady Victoria uneasily.

'He'll be fine,' said Kitty, her eyes going to the hunched-up figure of Tabitha, who was sobbing even more loudly.

'Tabitha, come here,' said Lady Victoria.

For a moment Kitty thought that Tabitha was going to ignore her aunt, but then she reluctantly dragged herself to her feet and came slowly across the terrace, her head hanging, the picture of woe.

'Tabitha, why did you try to strangle your little brother?' asked Lady Victoria severely.

'Because I hate him,' said Tabitha sulkily.

'What!' Lady Victoria's gasp of horror was genuine. 'I can't believe you said that, Tabitha. Your own little brother! You should love your little brother.'

'Well, I don't. I hate him,' said Tabitha. She turned away from her aunt, went back to her place in the corner and started to cry again.

Lady Victoria followed her. 'Well, Tabitha, you must be punished if you do bad things like that,' she said. 'I'm afraid that I can't take a badly behaved little girl like you to see your grandfather. I shall only take Robert with me. It's a pity, because I know your grandfather has a present ready for each of you, but little girls who try to strangle their little brothers can't expect to get presents. Come with me, Kitty; we'll leave this bad little girl alone.'

Lady Victoria swept off along the terrace. Kitty followed, looking uneasily back at Tabitha.

'I think she might be missing her father and mother, my lady,' she said in a low voice. 'That might be why she's behaving badly.'

'That's no excuse,' said Lady Victoria firmly. 'Robert is missing his father and mother too. He has a little cry occasionally, but that's understandable. Tabitha's behaviour is appalling.'

Kitty was silent. She thought uneasily of how sulky and bad-tempered she had been when she came to Drumshee. And I'm more than five years older than Tabitha, she thought.

'What happened to the children's parents, my lady?' she asked, and then wondered whether it was rude of her to cross-question an important person like Lady Victoria Fitzgerald.

'They both died of consumption,' said Lady Victoria, not seeming at all put out by the question. 'My sister-in-law was never well after Robert's birth, and she died a few years later. Then my brother sickened, and he died just a few months ago. The children have been staying with my elder sister in Cork, but she doesn't want to keep them. Her own children are grown up, and these two exhausted her with their continual fighting. We are hoping that their mother's brother in America might adopt them.'

Poor little things, thought Kitty. At least Uncle Mike and Aunt Maggie were delighted to have me at Drumshee.

Lady Victoria looked a little uneasy. Tabitha's sobs were even louder than before; they sounded quite heart-rending.

'Perhaps I should take her to visit her grandfather, after all,' Lady Victoria said, looking worried. 'The only thing is that that would mean going back on what I said, and I don't think one should do that with a child.'

Kitty nodded. She could see the sense in that, but she hated to think of Tabitha being left to cry for the afternoon while her brother went off in the motor car.

Suddenly she had an inspiration.

'When you take Master Robert to see his grandfather, could I take Miss Tabitha back to Drumshee with me for an hour?' she asked. 'She could come back with the man who drives the cart. It would be a little outing for her, and you would still be keeping your word.'

Lady Victoria's face cleared. 'That's a good idea — if you wouldn't mind, and your aunt and uncle wouldn't mind.' She turned to go; then she turned back and added, 'Oh, and Kitty — her grandfather has bought her a present: the most magnificent doll. You can tell her about it, as a secret, if you like, and say that she will be allowed to have it if she begs Master Robert's pardon for hurting him.'

CHAPTER FIVE

*W*hen Kitty arrived at Corofin House the following week, she could see that Tabitha had managed to apologise. The first sight that met her eyes was the little dark figure of Tabitha, holding the most enormous doll Kitty had ever seen. The doll's head was made of delicate porcelain; a wig of blond hair flowed down her back, and her eyelashes and eyebrows were made of real hair.

The first thing Tabitha said was 'How are the ducks?'

'The ducks are fine, Miss Tabitha,' said Kitty. 'Let me see your doll. Look at her lovely clothes!'

'She's got lace-trimmed drawers under her dress,' said Tabitha.

'She looks just like a picture of Queen Mary that I saw in the railway station in Liverpool,' said Kitty, examining the elegant doll's ankle-length silk dress.

'Grandpa has a picture of King George and Queen Mary in his drawing-room,' said Robert, coming out of the conservatory with a big wooden yacht in his hands.

'Oh, shut up about Grandpa,' said Tabitha viciously. 'If you say another word about Grandpa, I'll throw that stupid boat into the River Fergus, and it'll go sailing down to Ennis and down the Shannon and out to sea and you'll never see it again.'

'You're just jealous because you didn't go to see Grandpa,' said Robert stoutly, but Kitty noticed that he clutched the precious boat tightly to his chest, and that he had gone a little pale. He obviously believed that Tabitha was capable of carrying out her threat.

'Let me see your boat, Master Robert,' Kitty said hastily, taking the boat from him and holding it safely in her hands.

'It's got real sails on it, look!' said Robert. 'And real rigging, too. It's just like a real yacht. You can turn the sails around and move them up and down — and look, you can pull up this piece of wood and there's a little cabin underneath. Aunt Victoria says I can take it to America with me.'

'That's a good idea,' said Tabitha dreamily, almost as if she were talking to herself.

Robert looked at her suspiciously. 'What's a good idea?' he asked.

'I'll just throw your yacht over the rail of the ship, that'll be better than throwing it into the Fergus,' said Tabitha with a wicked smile.

Robert's face contorted, and he threw himself at his sister.

'Now, children,' said Kitty, hastily putting the yacht on the gravel and catching each child by the arm, 'don't fight, because I've just had a good idea. Master Robert, you pick up your yacht, and Miss Tabitha, you bring your doll, and we'll sit over on that bench and I'll tell you about my idea.'

They came with her, she was relieved to find, although Tabitha dragged her feet in the gravel, spoiling its neatly raked patterns and scuffing the toes of her shiny patent-leather shoes.

'Well,' said Kitty, 'Miss Tabitha's treat first, because she's the eldest. But before I tell you about the treat, you must both promise me that you'll try not to quarrel and that you'll try very hard to be good. Who's going to promise first?'

Out of the corner of her eye she could see that Robert had sat up, with his mouth just about to open, so she put in quickly: 'I think it should be Miss Tabitha, as she's the eldest.'

'I promise,' said Tabitha quickly. 'At least,' she added with a scowl, 'I'll promise if he tries not to be so annoying all the time.'

'And I promise, too,' said Robert, with an angelic smile.

'Well,' said Kitty, hoping desperately that rich children who had everything in the world would like her simple ideas, 'well, for Miss Tabitha's treat, we'll ask Lady Victoria if she will allow me to get some scraps of material from the dressmaker, and I'll stitch a whole wardrobe for your doll — ball dresses, walking suits, evening gowns, petticoats, bonnets, anything you like.'

'And a fur wrap like Aunt Victoria has?' asked Tabitha eagerly.

'If I can,' promised Kitty, thinking it would be worth anything to see such a happy smile on Tabitha's sulky little face.

'And what about my treat?' enquired Robert.

'Well,' said Kitty, inventing fast, 'how would you like it if I were to make you some sailors for your yacht? You could tell me what uniforms they should wear. And if I make the bodies out of pipe-cleaners, they'll be able to bend their legs and arms, so they can pull the rigging and all sorts of things like that,' she ended vaguely, not too sure exactly what went on in a yacht.

'And you could make him a flag, too,' observed Tabitha.

'Oh, that's a good idea, Tabby,' said Robert, his eyes shining with enthusiasm. 'A flag to put in the stern! That would be just perfect. Oh, here's Aunt Victoria — I'll go and tell her.'

He really is a sweet little boy, thought Kitty. It's no wonder everyone loves him. She took Tabitha's hand firmly in hers and whispered, 'Let's go and tell your aunt about the plans for your doll, Miss Tabitha, and I'll tell her how you've both promised to be so good.'

Lady Victoria, Kitty was relieved to see, was quite enthusiastic about the plans; she proposed that they should go straight down to the dressmaker and see what she had in the way of materials.

'If she hasn't got what you want,' she said generously, 'then we will buy some materials when we go to Ennis tomorrow. A beautiful lady doll like that needs the best of silks and satins and velvets for her clothes. And we might just be able to get some fur, Kitty. I have an old wrap which wasn't properly stored; the moth got at it, and I'll never wear it again. I have a new one now. You may have it if you wish.'

Tabitha glowed. She could be a very pretty little girl, thought Kitty. Lady Victoria obviously thought so too, because she smiled benignly at her little niece.

'What are you going to call your doll, Tabitha?'

Tabitha thought for a moment and then nodded her dark head. 'I'll call her Mary,' she said decisively. 'Kitty thinks she looks like Queen Mary.'

'What a good idea,' cried Lady Victoria. 'And if you're a very good girl, I might buy you a boy doll for Christmas. You could call him George, after the king.'

'I don't want a boy doll,' said Tabitha rudely. 'I hate boys.'

Oh dear, thought Kitty. She said hastily, 'Shall we walk down to the dressmaker now, my lady?'

'Oh, could we go in the Daimler?' pleaded Robert. 'I just love riding in it. Please, please, please!'

His aunt looked at him with a fond smile. 'Well, just for once, then,' she said. 'You run and find John. He can take you.'

Tabitha, scowling, busied herself with investigating the doll's frilly underwear, and her aunt gave her a slightly annoyed glance.

'Come with me, Kitty,' Lady Victoria said. 'I will give you some money to buy the material. Oh, and I think it might be a good idea if you purchased a sewing kit for yourself. You will know what you need.'

Within a few minutes, the big car drew up in front of the house, and Kitty and the children climbed into the luxurious leather seats.

'Thank you, John,' said Robert to the handsome young chauffeur, in a good imitation of Lady Victoria's gracious accents. 'We are ready now.'

He drew up the glass partition between the back and front seats, and then immediately let it down again and leaned into the front. 'I say, John,' he said eagerly, 'do you think you could teach me to drive this motor car? I'm sure I could. I've watched you.'

John chuckled. 'You'll have to get a bit bigger first, Master Robert,' he said. 'You'll need legs my size before you can do all this double de-clutching.'

Robert sank back in his seat. 'Double de-clutching,' he said, savouring the new word. Then he bounced up again. 'John, what's double de-clutching?'

'Well, it's what you do with the gear lever,' said John patiently, swinging the big car out of the gates and turning to go down the main street of Corofin. 'You need to change gear when you go up a big hill.'

'Like when we went to Grandpa's house?'

'I told you,' said Tabitha, through gritted teeth, 'shut up about Grandpa's house. I warned you.'

'Miss Tabitha, why don't you tell Master Robert all about Drumshee and what you did there?' said Kitty hastily.

Tabitha turned on Robert triumphantly. 'I had an absolutely marvellous time,' she said. 'Kitty's aunt gave me some stale bread and I fed all the ducks on the pond, and then we walked down to the river. It's the same River Fergus, but it's very small at Drumshee; it's only just risen from the lake. And then Kitty showed me a secret place, called a fort, where people used to live two thousand years ago. And then we crawled under a big tree that comes right down to the ground, and there was something there, all made of stone, that looked like a little toy church, and inside it was a stone doll called Saint Brigid, and we both knelt down and said a prayer. And guess what I made a wish for, when I said my prayer?' she added viciously.

'Here's the dressmaker's,' said Kitty quickly, dreading to hear what Tabitha had prayed for. 'I wonder whether she has any velvet, Miss Tabitha? I think a velvet dress is just what your doll needs.'

Fortunately the dressmaker did have some velvet, and many other luxurious materials. There won't be any need to go to Ennis, thought Kitty. Mrs Neylon was even able to sell her a neat sewing kit, with razor-sharp scissors and a set of needles of different sizes.

'And here's a nice piece of lawn,' she said enthusiastically. 'You'll be able to make a lovely nightgown for your doll out of that, Miss.'

Tabitha beamed, and even helped Robert to choose some bits of blue and white material for his sailors. For once, they seemed to be chatting happily. The visit was a great success.

As John helped Kitty to stow away the materials in the car's luggage-box, he said quietly, 'I wouldn't let the little girl go on too much about saying prayers to the statue of Saint Brigid. The Fitzgeralds are Church of Ireland. They're very against saints and the like.'

'Oh, dear,' said Kitty, biting her lip. 'I'll ask her to say nothing,' she decided. 'I'll tell her that it's a secret and Robert is too young for secrets.'

'Do that,' advised John, with a smile. 'You're a wonder with those two. Her ladyship was tearing her hair out before you came.'

Kitty laughed and got into the car. John's very nice, she thought; very handsome, too. She looked affectionately at the children. It was a funny thing, but ever since she had met the two Fitzgerald children she had stopped thinking about her own troubles.

I suppose I have enough to do, worrying about them, she thought. Well, at least there'll be so much for them to do on the ship, what with the swimming pool and other children to play with, that it should be a very peaceful trip.

CHAPTER SIX

They left Corofin very early on Tuesday morning. They would spend Tuesday night in Limerick, and Wednesday night in Cork with Lady Victoria's sister; then, at eleven o'clock on Thursday morning, they would board the *Titanic*.

Robert had a little notebook which his grandfather had given him; he had promised to write down everything that happened on the ship, and to draw pictures of everything he saw. On the first page he had already written, in large childish letters, '11 April 1912. We boarded the *Titanic* at 11.00.'

'I bet it'll be late, and then you'll have to rub that out,' Tabitha sniffed when she saw it; but even she was wildly excited by the idea of the journey, and she was pleasanter than usual to Robert.

Kitty, too, was glowing with excitement. Underneath her neat uniform and her brand-new travelling cape, she wore her gold necklace, hidden safely under her dress. Best of all, in her box was the beautiful pink velvet dress which had been found in the chimney cupboard at Drumshee.

'It does have a stain on the side — it could have been white wine,' Lady Victoria had said. 'It also looks much more worn than the others. So I think, my dear, that I will give it to you. I would like to give you a little present, as you have been so good with the children. You are so clever with your needle that you can alter it and make a nice party dress for yourself, to wear when you are older.'

Kitty smiled to herself. She knew that she wouldn't wait till she was too much older before she wore the dress. John, who was also going to America, had told her that there would be great parties every night on the *Titanic*, and Kitty planned to go to them whenever Lady Victoria could look after the children. The dress was almost a perfect fit. The skirt was much too wide for modern fashions, so Kitty had taken out a big panel on either side; now it looked like new, elegant and graceful.

Queenstown was a pretty town, full of gaily painted houses clustered around the harbour. As soon as they neared the quayside they could see the *Titanic*. Even though it was anchored two miles out, the ship looked enormous.

'They say it is more like a floating hotel than a ship,' said Lady Victoria, sounding almost as excited as the children.

'How are we going to get out there?' shrieked Robert, bouncing up and down on the soft leather seats of the Daimler.

'You'll have to swim,' said Tabitha.

'Don't be silly, dear,' said her aunt. 'And don't tease your brother. Look, Robert, those two little boats are the tenders. We will all go out on one of them. The *Titanic* is too big to come any closer.'

Tabitha was stiff with apprehension as they crossed the gangplank to the tender; but Robert — wearing his sailor suit, with his whistle around his neck, as usual — jumped in as if he were as used to the sea as any of the seamen. Several of the passengers smiled at him.

Kitty kept an eye on Tabitha. Her face had gone very white as soon as the boat cast off, and there were little drops of perspiration on her forehead.

'Come to the front of the boat with me, Miss Tabitha,' she said. 'The wind on your face will make you feel better.'

'You mean the *bows*, Kitty, not the front,' shouted Robert. 'This is the stern, and that's the bows, up there.'

Everyone smiled, and one of the seamen laughed out loud.

'Show-off,' said Tabitha, with an attempt at her usual snappy tones, but her heart wasn't in it.

She's going to be sick in a minute, thought Kitty. She frantically searched her mind for something to distract the little girl.

'What sort of a fur wrap would you like for the doll, Miss Tabitha?' she said hurriedly. 'Have a look at the ladies here and tell me which of their wraps you like best.'

'I think, really, that she needs a fur coat,' said Tabitha seriously, a little tinge of colour creeping back into her cheeks. 'It gets very cold at sea. I'm really shivering, and I've got my warmest coat on.'

'I'll try to make her a fur coat,' promised Kitty, inwardly groaning a little as she thought of stitching the stiff skins.

'And a muff, to keep her hands warm?'

'And a muff.'

Tabitha had a white fur muff of her own, slung around her neck with a dark green cord which matched her green wool coat. Inside the muff, though, her hands were still cold, Kitty noticed as the icy little fingers gripped hers.

'I wonder if your aunt will allow you to look at the ladies all dressed up for the balls,' she said. 'If she would, you could choose the fashion that you like for the doll's ball gown. We'll make it out of that pink velvet which the dressmaker gave us.'

'Stop calling her "the doll",' said Tabitha petulantly. 'Call her Mary.'

'Well, you see, I'm never sure whether to call her Mary or Queen Mary,' confessed Kitty. Or even Miss Mary, she thought.

'Let's call her Queen Mary, then,' said Tabitha. 'No, Princess Mary sounds nicer. Queens are old. We'll call her Princess Mary. I wish I had her with me now.'

'I'll unpack her as soon as you're in your cabin,' promised Kitty.

When they reached the *Titanic*, Tabitha looked quite frightened. The huge ship towered above the tender. Kitty had read that it was as tall as an eleven-story building, but it was only when she was right underneath it and looking up that she fully realised how big it was. She caught her breath with excitement. I'll never forget this trip, she thought, as they walked up the gangplank into the ship.

They followed the steward to the lift which would take them up to the first-class cabins.

'Imagine, Robert, a ship with a lift!' said Lady Victoria. 'You must tell your grandfather about that.'

'I hope we have a porthole in our cabin,' said Robert. 'That's a window, Kitty,' he added kindly.

The children's cabin opened out of their aunt's. There were two berths in it, and a cupboard for their clothes, and it did have a small porthole looking out on the sea. It was as pretty as a bedroom, but Tabitha and Robert were most interested in the porthole. There was a short, vicious struggle between them as to who should have the bed underneath it.

'I think Miss Tabitha should have it, as she is the eldest,' declared Kitty, and then felt rather ashamed. Really, Robert would value it more, as he was so interested in the sea and ships. I mustn't give in to Tabitha all the time, just because I'm afraid of her making a fuss, Kitty thought.

'... For the first night,' she finished. 'And then Master Robert will have it for the second night, and then you'll swap again. It will be much more fun than going to bed in the same place every night.'

Quickly she unpacked the rest of their clothes, gave Tabitha Princess Mary and Robert his yacht, and then went into the other cabin to see if Lady Victoria needed any help.

Lady Victoria's cabin was magnificent. Kitty smiled to herself, remembering her nightmare journey on the filthy ship which had brought her from Liverpool to Cork. This cabin had a four-poster bed, a dressing table, an electric heater, a marble bathroom between the two cabins, and a couple of luxurious armchairs. One of the stewardesses was unpacking Lady Victoria's clothes and putting them into drawers or hanging them in the large wardrobe.

Lady Victoria smiled when she saw Kitty.

'If you've finished the children's unpacking,' she said kindly, 'you may go and find your own cabin and do your own unpacking. Wait — I'll ring for a steward and get him to show you the way and carry your box down.'

The steward was a friendly fellow. He told Kitty that he was from Southampton and that he had only been working on the *Titanic* for a few days, since she had been launched.

'I've never seen a ship like her,' he said. 'The money they must have spent on her! They've even got real coal fires in some of the saloons and lounges. Real fires! I ask you! What a silly waste of money, when every room has electric heaters .... Let's go down the Grand Staircase. The maids' and valets' dining-room is down on the shelter deck; that's where you'll go for your meals. Your cabin is in third class. A bit mean, that, isn't it?'

'I suppose it would have cost more money for me to go first class, though,' pointed out Kitty.

'That's true,' admitted the steward. 'I've heard that some of those first-class passengers are paying eight hundred and fifty pounds for their suites. Can you imagine! You could buy a big house for that kind of money. The third-class fare is only nine pounds.'

'Nine pounds seems like a lot of money to me,' said Kitty. 'It's several months' wages for someone my age.'

Kitty thought the third-class cabin was fine. It was neat and clean and comfortable. There were four berths; the other three were occupied by a widow called Mrs Healy and her two daughters — Joan, who was about sixteen, and Maureen, who was Kitty's age.

'My other three daughters are out in America already,' Mrs Healy told Kitty. 'They're good girls. They all saved their wages and sent the money for me and the youngest two to come and join them.'

Kitty hung up her clothes and showed them the pink

velvet dress which Lady Victoria had given her.

'Oh, that's lovely! You can wear that at the céilí tonight,' said Joan.

'What's a céilí?' asked Kitty.

'Oh, it's a dance — jigs and reels and all sorts of music. It's great fun. You'll enjoy it. Will you come?'

'I will if Lady Fitzgerald allows me,' promised Kitty.

Luckily her ladyship was quite tired after the long journey from County Clare to Queenstown harbour, and the sea air was making her sleepy. Even more fortunately, Tabitha and Robert were exhausted after an afternoon of wildly running around the ship, and their eyes were shut as soon as their heads touched their pillows. Kitty promised to be up early in the morning, and was graciously given the evening off.

She got lost twice on her way to her cabin, but there was always some pleasant steward or stewardess at hand to help, and she arrived back in good time. She hoped that she had not eaten too much dinner to enjoy the dancing. I've never in my life seen as much food as there was on that table, she thought. If that's what the maids and valets get, goodness only knows what the menu in first class is like.

Mrs Healy and Maureen had already left for the céilí, but the elder girl, Joan, was still curling her hair.

'Oh, I'm so glad you're still here,' said Kitty. 'I don't know where the party is, or anything about it. I keep getting lost.'

'I'll wait for you,' said Joan good-naturedly. 'Are you really wearing that dress? It looks too good for a céilí.'

'Well, it's all I've got,' said Kitty. 'Except for this,

I've only got my uniforms and an old skirt and blouse.'

'You'll be the belle of the ball,' said Joan with good-natured envy. 'That gilt necklace looks shiny enough to be real gold. I suppose it's the light in here.'

'I suppose so,' said Kitty, struggling into the tight bodice of the dress. 'I'll just brush my hair and then I'll be ready.'

'You've got a lovely shine to your hair. Pity it doesn't curl, but you can always do that when you're older.'

'Let's go,' said Kitty, giving a satisfied glance at herself in the mirror. She was quite happy with her hair. She had no intention of frizzing it up and spoiling its glossy smoothness.

Patrick McMahon had taught his daughter all the Irish dances, so she was able to do a jig and take part in the reel as well as anyone who had been born and brought up in Ireland.

'You're a great dancer,' said John, as he swung her around and around. 'It's a pity we didn't know each other back home. My father plays the fiddle and my two brothers play the tin whistle, and we have céilís nearly every night of the week. Still, there'll be plenty of dancing on the *Titanic*. And who knows — you might be able to come up to Boston for a few days and stay with my sister. She says there's great craic there. The place is full of Irish.'

Kitty smiled into his brown eyes. She was looking forward to her time in America more and more.

CHAPTER SEVEN

*K*itty was yawning and her feet were sore as, next morning, she threaded her way through the innumerable passages of the *Titanic*. She snatched a hasty cup of tea and a sandwich in the maids' and valets' dining-room, and then hurried towards the first-class cabins. To her surprise, there was no sign of Lady Victoria or of the two children. Hastily she ran up the first-class staircase. She almost crashed into Lady Victoria, who was coming out of the Verandah and Palm Court, chatting to an equally elegant lady.

'Oh, good morning, Kitty,' she said affably. 'Are Miss Tabitha and Master Robert awake yet?'

Kitty gulped. 'They're not in their cabin, my lady,' she said nervously. I should have been up here earlier, she thought guiltily.

Lady Victoria frowned. 'Those bad children,' she said to her companion. 'I told them distinctly last night that they were never to leave their cabin unless either I or Kitty was with them. They are such a responsibility, my dear. You have no idea what they are like. Well, I must leave you and go and find them. Perhaps we will meet at eleven for coffee?'

'I'm sorry, my lady,' said Kitty. 'I should have been up earlier. I got lost coming here.' That's partly true, anyway, she thought.

'Nonsense, my dear, it's quite early. I shouldn't have left them, perhaps, but they were sleeping so soundly, and I felt so wakeful that I thought I would take a turn on the boat deck; and then I met Lady Cooper and we decided to breakfast together.'

They had reached the cabins, but there was no sign of the children.

'I'll run and look in the dining saloon and the lounge, my lady,' said Kitty.

'Do,' said Lady Victoria. 'I'll ring for the steward and get him to look as well.'

There was no sign of the children in either of the dining-rooms, or in the lounge.

Kitty went up on the boat deck and walked around it, dodging gentlemen in overcoats and caps and ladies in ankle-length fur coats, with felt hats pulled well down over their ears to protect them against the cold wind. There was no sign of the children. Coming back, Kitty met a steward calling out in an embarrassed way: 'Miss Tabitha, Master Robert, where are you?' He gave her a wink, and she knew how ridiculous he felt. Still, he was paid to give satisfaction to the first-class passengers, and whether that meant exercising their dogs or hunting for their children, he would do it.

Kitty smiled to herself. It was silly, really. When I was Tabitha's age, she thought, I was running around the streets of Liverpool. My mother was working and I had a key tied around my neck. I came home when I was hungry or tired or cold, and I felt lucky — not many of the other children were trusted with a key ....

'Perhaps they're in the gymnasium,' said the steward, coming back.

'I'll try there, if you'll look on the promenade deck,' Kitty said.

There were quite a few ladies and gentlemen in the gymnasium, riding on electric camels, rowing non-existent boats or cycling stationary bicycles; but there was no sign of Tabitha and Robert. Kitty came out and looked around helplessly. On the promenade deck she could hear the steward still calling, and below, on the upper deck, another steward took up the call.

They're probably hiding somewhere, little monkeys, thought Kitty; but despite herself, she was beginning to get slightly uneasy. It was hard to be sure what Tabitha would do if she were in a rage with Robert. Suddenly she thought of Tabitha's words, back in Corofin House: 'I'll just throw your yacht over the rail of the ship.' What if Tabitha had carried out her threat? What if Robert had tried to stop her?

Quickly Kitty clattered down the first-class staircase, too worried to stand politely aside for several ladies who were coming up, chatting to one another. She dived between them and went on running, as fast as she could, down to the cabins.

Lady Victoria was still there, looking quite worried. Kitty went past her without a word of explanation, opened the children's toy-box, and found her worst fears confirmed. The doll, Princess Mary, lay there in all her splendour, but there was no sign of Robert's yacht.

Kitty turned and ran out of the cabin. Her mind was working furiously. The children were not on the first-class decks; she could still hear the voices of the two stewards calling them. There might be a chance,

though, that they had run down to the third-class deck, towards the front of the ship. As Kitty ran, she could almost hear Robert's little voice saying, 'not the front, Kitty, the bows'. Her eyes filled with tears. She hoped desperately that nothing had happened to either of the children. If it has, she thought, I'll never forgive myself for being late.

Quickly she clattered down the iron steps to the third-class deck. In her hurry, her foot caught on the last step; she slipped, overbalanced, and almost fell. An arm caught her.

'Kitty!' laughed John. 'You'll break your neck! You should come down these stairs a bit more carefully. They're not like your fancy first-class staircase. What's the matter with you, anyway? You're as white as a ghost.'

'Oh, John,' said Kitty, clutching at him, 'the two children are missing! We've searched everywhere ....'

John looked at her with amusement. 'They'll turn up,' he said. 'They're probably off playing hide-and-seek somewhere. That pair are always up to mischief.'

'I hope so,' said Kitty, beginning to feel a little better. It was possible that they were hiding. They might be snuggled behind one of the sixteen lifeboats on the boat deck, stifling their giggles as they listened to all the calling. She smiled a little.

'That's better,' said John. 'You're getting your colour back. Don't worry too much about those children. There's too much fussing over them.'

'I suppose so,' said Kitty uncertainly. Then a thought struck her and she felt cold all over again.

'Yes, but John,' she said, 'they've taken Robert's yacht. They wouldn't have done that if they were just going to play hide-and-seek.' She hesitated for a moment, wondering whether to tell him about Tabitha's threat to throw the yacht overboard.

John, however, was laughing. 'That's it, then,' he said. 'The little monkeys! I know where they've gone. Master Robert was telling me about the swimming pool and how he was going to sail his boat on it. That's where they'll be. Come on. I'll go down with you. You'll never find it yourself — this ship is like a maze. Let's go down these steps here.'

Down they went — one flight, and then another, and another, and another. The steps were steep and difficult — more like ladders than staircases, really. Kitty thought they would never get to the swimming pool. She half-wished that she had gone back to the first-class deck and gone down by the lift. Still, she did feel much better now that she was with John; he was so relaxed and amused.

'How many more flights?' she asked.

'There are twelve of them altogether,' said John. 'I was having a look around this morning, trying to get my bearings. I went down and had a look at the boilers. The stokers get great money, but it's a bad job. They have to work in about a hundred degrees of heat. The sweat just pours off them. I'm hoping they'll teach me a bit about how the boilers work. I might get a job with boilers when I get to America.'

'You're definitely not coming back to Ireland, then?' asked Kitty, conscious of a feeling of disappointment edging out her worry over the children.

The black curly head in front of her shook vigorously from side to side. 'No, I'm not,' John said emphatically. 'There's nothing for me in Ireland. I don't want to be a servant to rich people for the rest of my life. I'm going to make some money for myself. What about you?' he called back over his shoulder, as they went around another corner and climbed onto yet another ladder.

'I'm going back,' said Kitty. 'I'm going to live with my uncle and aunt at Drumshee and be apprenticed to the dressmaker in Corofin.'

'Well, maybe you'll come out to America when you've finished your apprenticeship?' suggested John. 'I'll give you my address and you can write to me. I'll be staying with my sister in Boston. If you come out, you can stay with her until you find your own place. It's nice to do that. You wouldn't want to be all alone in a strange country.'

'Thank you,' said Kitty shyly. 'I'll write to you, anyway,' she added. 'I'll send you all the news from Ireland.'

Would I like to go to America in a few years' time? she wondered. A feeling of excitement came over her. I think I would, she decided.

Then a feeling of shame overcame her excitement. It was terrible to be feeling so happy when those two children were missing and she didn't know what had happened to them!

Aloud she said, 'How many more flights, John?'

'Just another two,' he called back. 'Then we'll just sprint down the firemen's passage and through a boiler-room, and then up a few flights and we'll be there. Look in there; that's where the motor cars are. Down the next flight is where most of the cargo is.'

'It's like going down to the bottom of the earth,' said Kitty. 'Or like going down to hell,' she added, remembering a picture which she had once seen of the damned going down a long ladder into the flames of hell.

More like going down to hell, actually, she thought a few minutes later, as they ran through the boiler-room. The place was terribly hot, and the flames of the boilers roared and leaped. John called out a greeting to a man with a face black with coal dust, who was stoking the fire in one of the boilers; then he tried to tell Kitty something, but she could not hear him. She felt on fire with the intense heat, and the noise was so great that she thought her head would burst if she did not get out quickly.

When they burst through the swing doors at the end of the boiler-room, Kitty drew a deep breath. She had never realised how dreadful noise and heat could be.

'My father worked in the mines,' she told John. 'I suppose it must have been like that. I don't know how he stood it.'

'Well, you earn good money doing it,' said John. 'You could earn more money in a week there than you'd get in a year out in the mud and the dirt and the rain in dear old County Clare.'

I'd prefer rain and dirt to heat and noise, Kitty thought. She remembered the clean salt-laden wind blowing her hair as she had stood in the fields of Drumshee, and she began to feel a bit homesick.

'Please, Saint Brigid, help me to find those children and I'll never take my eyes off them for the rest of the time,' she muttered, thinking of the little shrine under the old ash tree.

'Here we are — the swimming pool,' said John, pushing open a door.

For a moment Kitty thought there was nobody there. The huge pool, as big as the whole of the cottage at Drumshee, lay before her, its water so clear that she could see the deep blue tiles at the bottom. The dressing-boxes at the side all stood open and empty. No, there was no one there ....

But then a little voice shouted, 'Kitty, come and look how well my yacht sails!' And there at the bottom of the swimming pool Kitty could just see two little figures, crouched over the side of the pool, while the white-sailed yacht bobbed on the blue water.

CHAPTER EIGHT

'*I* can't trust you children out of my sight for a moment,' said Lady Victoria crossly, hiding her relief under a show of severity. 'You will stay here in your cabin for the rest of the morning, and Kitty will have to stay with you. I will have lunch sent down to you, and then, if Kitty tells me that you have been very good, I might take you for a walk on the boat deck while Kitty has her lunch.'

Behind Lady Victoria's back, Tabitha made a face and stuck out her tongue. At least she and Robert are getting on better now, thought Kitty. Neither of the children had blamed the other for their escapade; each one had claimed that it had been his or her idea to go and sail the yacht on the swimming pool.

'Don't leave them alone for a moment, Kitty,' said Lady Victoria, in a low voice, as she prepared to go and meet her friends in the Café Parisien. 'We must make sure that one or the other of us is with them all the time. I must say, I will be pleased to get them off my hands. My brother-in-law has a family of his own; he will be able to cope with them better than I can.'

Poor little things, thought Kitty, as she turned to look at the two downcast faces.

'I've got a good idea to pass the morning,' she said cheerfully. 'Master Robert, I want you to draw a map of the ship in your notebook. Your grandfather will be so pleased! I can help you with the third-class bits — and guess what? John took me down to the boiler-room, and I saw the place where the cars are stored, so I can tell you where that is as well.'

Perhaps I shouldn't have said that, she thought, as Robert's face blazed with excitement. He'll be trying to go down to the boiler-rooms next.

The drawing was a good idea, though. Instantly Robert settled down with his notebook and his pencil, and with the well-handled leaflet about the *Titanic* which was one of his most precious possessions.

Tabitha watched him for a while and then got bored.

'What will I do?' she demanded.

'Shall we make a dress for your doll?' asked Kitty. 'I mean, for Princess Mary,' she hastily amended.

Tabitha brightened up. 'I know,' she said. 'We'll make her a swimming costume. When we first came down to the swimming pool, there was a lady just climbing out of the water. She stood under one of the spray things before she went into the box to dress, so I had time to have a good look at her costume. It was made of blue-and-white-striped material, and it only went as far as her knees, and she had a scarf around her head. I'll draw it for you and you can make it.'

'Right,' said Kitty. She went to sort through her bag of materials, praying that she would find some striped material and that they would have a peaceful morning.

Luckily there was a nice big piece of blue-and-white material, which Tabitha was pleased to say was just right. Together they designed the pattern; then Kitty threaded a needle with white cotton and gave a strip of the material to Tabitha.

'There,' she said. 'You can make the scarf to go around her head, Miss Tabitha.'

Tabitha stared in amazement. 'I can't sew,' she said. 'I'm much too young.'

'No, you're not,' said Kitty cheerfully. Isn't she spoilt, she thought. Imagine not being able to sew at nine years old! I suppose it's because her mother died when she was so young. No one has really tried to bring her up properly.

'I'll teach you,' she said aloud. 'I learned to sew when I was three years old.'

'You must have been a very clever little girl, then,' said Tabitha seriously, and Kitty had to tighten her lips to hide a smile.

'I'll pin it for you, and then all you need to do is stick the needle in and out. Try not to prick your finger, but don't worry if you do — I always did when I first started.'

What with the sewing and the drawing, the cabin was quiet and busy. The morning passed so quickly that Kitty could hardly believe the time when the steward arrived, bringing three trays.

'Her ladyship says that she hopes you don't mind eating here with the children,' he said to Kitty. 'She's met some friends, and she'll be delayed over lunch.'

'I don't mind,' said Kitty, her eyes widening at the sight of the heavily laden tray meant for her. 'What on earth is that?' she added, pointing at a plate of something that, to Kitty, looked like black slugs' eggs.

'That's caviar,' said the steward.

Kitty looked at it doubtfully. 'Try it, Kitty,' said Robert, in his most grown-up manner. 'I had a taste at Grandpa's house.' He gave a sidelong glance at Tabitha when he said 'Grandpa's house', but she was too interested in her sewing to get annoyed.

'We'll all share everything,' decided Kitty. 'You can have a taste of anything from my tray that you like the look of, and I'll have a taste of anything from your trays that looks nice. I think your apple pie looks nicer than this frothy stuff.'

'That's *oranges en surprise*,' said the steward loftily.

I'm not taking any nonsense from him, thought Kitty. Uncle Mike would laugh his head off at this fellow.

'Thank you, my man,' she said authoritatively. 'Just leave those trays on the table and tell her ladyship that the children are quite happy and that she should stay as long as she wants.'

After lunch the work resumed. Tabitha was really getting the hang of the sewing. She had neat little fingers and seemed to get a lot of satisfaction out of making things for her beloved doll. The swimming costume and the scarf were finished, and Princess Mary was dressed up in them; she didn't look quite as elegant as she did in her long gowns, but she was very presentable.

The doll was beautifully made. Her head and hands were made of china — Lady Victoria called it 'bisque' — and her body was made of very fine, soft kidskin, which looked and felt almost like real skin.

'What will we make next?' demanded Tabitha.

'What about a wrap to keep her warm after her swim?' suggested Kitty. 'I think you're good enough at sewing to do that yourself, Miss Tabitha. I'll cut it out for you and you can make it all by yourself.'

Kitty quickly cut out the wrap and threaded a needle for Tabitha. Then she went over to have a look at Robert's drawing.

'That's really good,' she said with sincerity. Robert

had worked on the map all morning, and it really was a remarkable piece of work for a seven-year-old.

'Look, Kitty, I've marked the decks in different colours,' he said. 'That's the boat deck where the lifeboats are, right at the top, and under that is the promenade deck — that bit there is the closed-in part, where people go on windy days, and those are the windows in it. And this one under the promenade deck is the bridge deck, and under that is the shelter deck, and then the saloon deck and the upper deck, and then there's the middle deck — where the swimming pool is,' he added, glancing guiltily at Kitty. 'And right at the bottom there's the lower deck.'

Kitty nodded and smiled, her eyes on Tabitha. I've never seen her look so contented, she thought.

Robert nudged her. 'Where's your cabin, Kitty?' he asked. 'Look, I've marked our cabins here.'

Kitty thought for a moment. 'Well, that's the poop deck, there, at the back of the boat — I mean the stern,' she hastily corrected herself. 'And underneath is the third-class smoking-room. You go down two flights of stairs there, and then my cabin is just here; it's the first on the right-hand side as you come down the stairs.'

Robert bent his blond head over the page; with the tip of his tongue sticking out of his mouth, he carefully drew an arrow and wrote, in small neat letters, 'Kitty's cabin'.

At that moment, the door opened and Lady Victoria came into the scene of industry. She was flushed and excited-looking; Kitty could smell the sweet wine on her breath and guessed that she had had a good lunch. Her crossness seemed to have evaporated. She admired the map and Princess

Mary's swimming costume, and even went so far as to say that Tabitha's sewing was better than her own and that she would buy her a little sewing-box when they reached America.

'And, Kitty,' she said, 'could I ask you to take the children for their walk around the deck? The ladies with whom I had lunch would like me to take a little promenade around the boat deck with them. I thought I should just run down and see how you were all getting on.'

'I'll be very pleased to, my lady,' said Kitty sincerely. The children are calm and happy now, she thought. Lady Victoria's very kind to them, really, but she does seem to get them restless and irritable. They'll be better with me.

'Take your fur coat, Aunt Victoria,' said Robert, with his grown-up air. 'You might get a chill on deck otherwise. This ship is going really fast.'

Lady Victoria smiled and kissed the two children; she caught up her fur coat and was gone in a moment, leaving a wave of expensive perfume behind her.

'Let's go on the poop deck, Kitty — oh please, Kitty,' begged Robert, as they came to the top of the Grand Staircase. 'I've never been on the poop deck. I've been on all the other decks. Oh please, please, please, Kitty — dear, good, kind, nice Kitty!'

Kitty hesitated. Lady Victoria had told her not to bring the children down to the third-class quarters, in case there might be some rough men about, but she wasn't sure whether that included the poop deck or not. She looked across. The poop deck was deserted, except for a few sailors busily winding ropes, and Captain Smith and one of his officers strolling up and down, talking quietly.

That decided her. If the captain was there, then it should be all right. 'Let's go across, then,' she said.

It's Friday now, thought Kitty, as they climbed up the ladder to the poop deck. In a few more days we'll be in New York .... The *Titanic* was beginning to seem almost like a home to her; she could not imagine leaving it.

The sea was calm, and the deck felt steady. Kitty leaned on the railing and looked back at the ship.

Tabitha, for once, was in a sunny mood; she was walking Princess Mary up and down the deck, talking in low tones to the doll. She's really a sweet little girl, thought Kitty. It's a shame that no one takes any notice of her, while Robert is always being petted and admired.

Robert was hanging onto the rails, cupping one hand around his eye as if it were a telescope. 'Ship ahoy!' he called out in his clear, bell-like voice. A few of the sailors nearby smiled at him, and even the white-bearded captain looked across and laughed.

Tabitha's right, really, thought Kitty. Robert is a little show-off.

Robert knew everyone was looking at him; he left the railings and jumped lightly onto a big, flat-topped box on the deck. He put his whistle between his lips and blew an ear-piercing blast.

'Man the lifeboats, men,' he shouted.

'Now then, sonny, I give the orders around here,' said the captain. To Kitty's relief, he was laughing.

'And come down off that box,' he added. 'That's where the life-jackets are kept. We wouldn't want that box damaged, would we?'

'No, sir,' said Robert, and saluted. He had a sunny smile on his face and was in no way disconcerted. He jumped lightly off the box and saluted again.

'Are you going to be a sailor when you grow up, then?' asked the captain, smiling indulgently.

'Yes, sir,' said Robert, without a trace of shyness.

'Is this your first time at sea?' asked Captain Smith. Kitty could see that he was quite charmed by this little blond angel.

Robert shook his head. 'Oh, no,' he said. 'I've been to sea with my cousin Dominic, in his yacht. I helped him with his sails. It was really exciting. The sea was ever so rough — choppy, I mean. The yacht nearly turned over, and Tabby, my sister, was sick all over Dominic's shoes, and his trousers too,' he added.

'I'll kill you!' cried Tabitha, her voice rising to a shriek. 'I'll really kill you this time!' She dropped her doll on the deck, seized the cord of Robert's whistle, and twisted it so viciously that Robert's scream was almost throttled in his throat.

'Now then, young lady, don't do that!' The captain's roar boomed out like a foghorn, and several ladies who had been taking an after-dinner stroll on the boat deck came to the railings and looked down.

Kitty rushed across, seized Tabitha's hands and gave her a little shake. Then, looking up, she saw the stately figure of Lady Victoria Fitzgerald amongst the interested crowd on the boat deck. Kitty's heart sank. Lady Victoria said nothing, but she lifted one exquisitely gloved finger and beckoned.

Feeling as if she would like the deck to open up and swallow her, Kitty seized the sobbing Robert with her other hand and, as bravely as she could, started on the journey up to the boat deck.

Lady Victoria's face was stern.

'It's no good crying and saying you are sorry now, Tabitha,' she said severely. 'You will go straight to bed and stay there for the rest of the day. You will have only bread and milk for your supper — you deserve no more. And I am taking your doll away. I shall give it to Kitty, to put in her cabin, and you will not see it again until we reach New York.'

Tabitha burst into frantic weeping. Through her sobs she managed to cry out, 'She's my doll! You can't take her away! Oh, please, Aunt Victoria, I want her — she's *mine* ....'

'Tabitha, that is quite enough!' said Lady Victoria sharply. 'You heard what I said. Kitty, put Miss Tabitha to bed, please. But first, take the doll and put it in your box, in your cabin, at once.'

CHAPTER NINE

*B*y Sunday morning, Tabitha was still subdued and listless. Kitty had been to mass with the third-class passengers; when she arrived at the first-class quarters, Lady Victoria and the two children were just emerging from the service in the lounge.

'Shall I take the children for a walk on the boat deck, my lady?' Kitty asked.

'Yes, please, Kitty,' said Lady Victoria, in tones of such heartfelt relief that Kitty guessed that the children had fidgeted, or worse, right through the service. 'You had better put on their coats,' she added. 'It is turning very cold.'

Kitty took the children down to their cabin and got out their coats. Robert put on a smart little reefer jacket, which he buttoned over his sailor suit — tucking his whistle carefully inside, Kitty noticed with amusement. He obviously did not trust Tabitha not to have another go at strangling him.

Tabitha sat on her bed, hanging her head, and made no effort to get dressed. Kitty got her coat out of the wardrobe and looked at the little girl in a worried way. Tabitha was more devoted to Princess Mary than anyone could have suspected. Perhaps, thought Kitty, it's because her dead mother's father gave it to her. Tabitha must remember her mother. After all, she was about four years old when her mother died, while Robert would only have been two.

'Are you feeling sick, Miss Tabitha?' she asked

gently. Tabitha shook her head and stood up, holding out her arms and allowing the coat to be buttoned onto her. That shade of green doesn't suit her, thought Kitty. Who on earth bought it for her? She looks positively yellow in it.

She stretched out her hand and carefully felt the child's forehead. No, Tabitha didn't have a fever; she was quite cool.

'You'll feel better when we go on deck,' she said aloud. 'The wind will blow the cobwebs away.'

There wasn't really much wind on deck, but it certainly was cold — so cold that they all shivered. The sea was very calm, too, so Tabitha couldn't be seasick. She must just be missing her doll, Kitty thought. She made up her mind that she would plead with Lady Victoria to give the doll back to Tabitha. Lady Victoria was quite a kind woman, really, and Kitty had seen her give many worried glances at Tabitha's pale face.

'Let's walk to the bridge,' she said aloud.

Captain Smith was on the bridge. One of his officers approached him and handed him a piece of paper. 'Another ice warning,' Kitty heard him say, as the captain put the piece of paper in his pocket.

'Good morning, Captain Smith,' shouted Robert, saluting smartly as he loved to do.

'Good morning, Robert,' said Captain Smith with a smile. 'Good morning ....' He glanced at Tabitha, as if wondering what her name was, but she gave him a glance of such hatred that he quickly turned back to Robert.

'How's your ship today?' asked Robert, as bold as brass.

The captain's laugh boomed out, making several people turn around and smile in response.

'She's going very well, young sir,' he said with amusement. 'I hope you're pleased with her.'

'How many knots is she travelling at?' demanded Robert.

'Robert!' exclaimed Kitty, but the captain was still amused.

'Mr Lightoller, tell this young gentleman how many knots we're travelling at,' he ordered one of the officers.

'Twenty-two knots, sir.' The officer saluted Robert.

'Pretty good,' said Robert condescendingly. 'I'll write that in my notebook that I'm going to post to my Grandpa when we get to America.'

'Come on, Master Robert,' said Kitty hurriedly. 'We must go now. The captain is too busy to be talking to a little boy like you.'

Robert pouted a little as she hurried him away. He does love to be the centre of attention, thought Kitty. I'm sure it isn't good for him.

'Tell me what a knot is,' she said, to distract him.

Robert recovered his good humour. 'A knot is like a mile,' he said earnestly. 'My cousin Dominic told me that. It means that in an hour's time we'll be about twenty-two miles from here. Where are we, Kitty, do you think? It's really cold, isn't it? Maybe we're going to the North Pole.'

'I want to go back to the cabin,' said Tabitha, breaking her silence for the first time.

'Let's just go once around the boat deck, and then we'll go,' coaxed Kitty. 'Or I'll tell you what we'll do: we'll go into the library and find a book, and I'll read to the two of you. It will be nice and warm in the library. It's got lots of heaters in it.'

However, the library proved to have no children's books, so Kitty got Robert a periodical about sailing and handed Tabitha a book of ladies' fashions. Robert promptly buried himself in the pictures of yachts and rigging, but Tabitha only gave the book of fashions a cursory glance before pushing it aside.

'Tell me a story about Drumshee,' she said, snuggling in against Kitty.

Kitty searched her mind for something that she could tell Tabitha about Drumshee.

'I love Drumshee,' said Tabitha dreamily. 'When we come back from America, I'm going to come and live with you and baby Bridget at Drumshee. I'll help you look after Bridget, and I'll sew clothes for her.' She looked up at Kitty and frowned. 'We are coming back, Kitty, aren't we?' she asked.

Kitty listened with a feeling of shock. Was it possible that the children didn't know they were going to stay in America? They're passed from house to house like a parcel of books, she thought. She tried to think of something to distract Tabitha, so that she would not have to answer the question.

'I've thought of a story about Drumshee,' she said. 'Shall I tell it to you?'

Tabitha nodded, so eager to hear the story that she forgot all about her question.

'Well,' Kitty began, 'once upon a time, there was a very, very poor girl who lived at Drumshee. She wanted to be a very rich girl, and she didn't know what to do. But then, one day, a rainbow came to Drumshee — the most beautiful rainbow in the world. And right underneath the old ash tree, the girl saw a leprechaun — that's a little fairy man. "Dig at the foot of the rainbow," said the leprechaun. "If you do that, you will find a pot of gold ....'"

Kitty went on and on, inventing the most wonderful things she could think of. Robert had allowed the periodical to drop to the ground, and Tabitha's sallow cheeks were flushed with excitement.

'... And a thick grey mist came down over the valley of the little River Fergus, and the leprechaun was never seen again at Drumshee,' Kitty finished, an hour later. Robert had fallen asleep in a corner of the sofa, but Tabitha was cuddled against Kitty, eyes shining, cheeks pink with excitement.

'You tell lovely stories, Kitty,' she whispered. 'You tell stories just like my Mama used to do.'

'Do you remember her?' asked Kitty, stroking the dark curls.

Tabitha nodded. 'I wish she would come back. I'm miserable without Mama and Papa.'

'My father and mother are dead, too,' said Kitty gently, not quite sure whether that was the right thing to say.

'And are you miserable without them?'

Kitty nodded. 'A bit,' she said. 'But not so much now that I'm looking after you,' she added truthfully.

Tabitha smiled. 'I'm not so miserable now that you're looking after me, either,' she said. 'Would you like me to tell you a bit about my Mama? Robert doesn't really remember her, but I do.'

'Yes,' said Kitty, and pulled the warm little body closer to her side. 'I'd like that very much.'

'You see,' said Kitty that night, as she and Lady Victoria stood looking down at the two sleeping children, 'I think the doll is very important to her, because she doesn't feel as if she has anything much belonging to her. She misses her father and mother terribly. I was surprised at how much she remembers about her mother, even though she was so young. And I think she's jealous of Robert — I mean, Master Robert — because everyone takes to him so quickly. She probably thinks that he gets more attention than she does for that reason,' Kitty finished, rather red in the face and not quite sure exactly what she meant herself.

However, Lady Victoria was nodding and not looking annoyed. 'Well, you are probably right,' she said. 'I'll give the doll back to her tomorrow. You can bring it up after breakfast. Oh, and Kitty — could I ask a favour of you? Some people from Philadelphia have asked me to a little party tonight. I don't know what time I will be back, and I certainly don't want to leave the children alone, so I wonder whether you would stay with them. I have asked the steward to make up a camp-bed here for you, so you can stay until the morning if I should happen to be late. Will that be all right?'

'Yes, of course,' said Kitty. She's really very nice, she thought. She always asks, instead of ordering.

'Well, have a peaceful night,' said Lady Victoria. She swept out, her silk cocktail dress swinging around her as she turned.

CHAPTER TEN

*I*t is peaceful, thought Kitty. She was quite tired. There had been a great céilí in the third-class dining-room the night before. Kitty had worn her pink dress and her gold necklace, and John had told her that she was the prettiest girl he had ever seen. They had danced together for most of the evening, and he had explained all his plans for getting rich in America. There would be no céilís or dancing that night, though, as it was Sunday.

Kitty sat down on the camp-bed which the steward had brought in, and decided that it was just as comfortable as her own bed in the third-class cabin. She undressed and lay down. The two children were still sleeping soundly. Kitty closed her eyes and fell asleep, forgetting to turn off the lights.

It was a bump, and a queer scraping sound, which woke her up. Her eyes went to the clock on the wall. It was a quarter to twelve. The door to Lady Victoria's cabin was still open; she wasn't back from her party yet. Kitty had just decided that she must have dreamt the bump when she heard voices in the corridor. Winding a blanket around herself and pushing her hair back from her face, she went to the door.

'Don't worry, ladies,' one of the stewards was saying. 'I'll just come around and close the portholes. It's getting very cold. We're getting near an ice field; that's what's lowered the temperature.'

An ice field, thought Kitty. She remembered the

officer's words to the captain that morning: 'Another ice warning ....' She sat on the edge of the bed and dressed herself quickly, pulling on the warm long black stockings and putting her new flannel-lined cape on the bed beside her.

The children had not stirred. Kitty went to the door of the cabin and listened as hard as she could. A man came out of his cabin, fully dressed, but with the legs of his pyjamas showing from under his trousers. There seemed to be more noise and more doors opening and closing than usual.

That decided her. Moving quietly, so as not to disturb the children, Kitty sorted out clothes for them to wear — warm underclothes, heavy woollen jumpers, the thickest stockings she could find, and high leather button-boots.

She placed their coats next to the piles. She looked at the clock again; it was five minutes past twelve. She went to the cabin door and looked up and down the corridor. There was no one there, but Kitty could hear the sound of hurrying feet on the floor above.

Not sure what to do, Kitty closed the door. At that moment, a little pile of marbles which Robert had left on top of the dressing table, next to his notebook, rolled to the edge of the table, fell to the floor, then rolled rapidly down the cabin and towards the side of the ship, ending up under the porthole.

Kitty stared at them for a moment before she realised the significance of what she had seen. The ship was leaning over to one side and dipping towards the front.

Quickly she made her decision. There was no danger, of course — the *Titanic* was unsinkable; but she dared not take a chance.

'Wake up, Miss Tabitha. Wake up, Master Robert,' she said quietly, leaning over their beds.

Tabitha woke instantly, her dark eyes full of apprehension.

'What's the matter, Kitty?' she asked, her voice loud with fear.

'Is it a lifeboat drill?' asked Robert, coming awake in an instant as he always did.

'Yes,' said Kitty, thankfully seizing on the explanation. 'You must get dressed in your warmest clothes. It's very cold outside.'

'I was wondering why we didn't have a lifeboat drill after the service this morning,' said Robert, cheerfully pulling on his knee-length black stockings and buttoning up his boots. 'My book about ships says that the captain always calls a lifeboat drill on Sunday morning. I wonder why Captain Smith didn't do that, Kitty.'

'I suppose he thought it might be more exciting at night,' said Kitty, pulling a second warm jumper over Tabitha's head and then buttoning her into her green coat.

'We'll need our life-jackets,' said Robert authoritatively. 'You must attend the drill wearing a life-jacket. They're on top of the cupboard, Kitty. Can you reach them down?'

It took Kitty a while to sort out the backs and fronts of the white canvas cork-filled life-jackets, and she had only just finished tying the tapes when the door opened and Lady Victoria came in, pale and worried.

'You are wonderful, Kitty,' she said warmly when

she saw the two children. 'I think I will follow your example and put on my life-jacket. The steward tells me that there is a slight problem. Nobody seems to be sure exactly what has happened, and certainly there is no reason to worry, but all the same .... Now, what do you think — over my fur coat or under it? Which would be the least clumsy?'

'Kitty needs a life-jacket, too,' said Robert.

'So she does. What a thoughtful boy! Steward!' Lady Victoria went to the door and called imperiously, and a steward came running. 'Ah, good — you have some spare life-jackets. May I have one for my maid? Thank you so much.'

Kitty fastened her life-jacket. She felt very thankful that Lady Victoria had come down to the cabin. Now, she thought, I'll just have to do what I'm told; I won't have to make any decisions.

'I'd better take my notebook and pencil,' said Robert. 'I want to write down things about the lifeboat drill for Grandpa. He'll be very interested. Could you stick it in my pocket, Kitty, please? I can't get at it with this life-jacket.'

'Let's go now. Children, you walk ahead,' said Lady Victoria. 'No, Robert, we'll leave the lights on, and the heaters too, so that it will be nice and warm when we come back to our cabin. Go ahead, Tabitha, dear; hold Robert's hand. We'll all go up onto the promenade deck and find out what is happening.'

There was only a little cluster of people on the promenade deck, not the crowds that Kitty had expected. The captain, looking worried, was talking in a low voice to one of the men.

'That's Mr Andrews. He built the ship,' whispered

Lady Victoria to Kitty. 'I suppose he and the captain will have to decide if there is any damage. I must say, I hope we don't have to go on those lifeboats. I would feel much safer on the ship.'

The captain and Mr Andrews went off down the Grand Staircase. Everyone else stayed on the deck, looking around uncertainly. Nobody seemed to be giving any orders. From the first-class lounge came the sound of jolly ragtime tunes.

'I'm cold,' said Tabitha abruptly. 'I want to go back to the cabin.'

'Not now, dear,' said Lady Victoria absently. Kitty could see that she was straining her ears to hear what one officer was saying to another. Several men started to drift away.

'Could you just go and look at the clock in the first-class lounge, Kitty, dear?' said Lady Victoria. 'Unfortunately my watch seems to have stopped.'

The band was still playing in the lounge when Kitty opened the door. In the far corner, four men sat playing cards and sipping whiskey. So nothing too serious can have happened, Kitty thought, or they wouldn't be sitting here so calmly.

'Oh, bother — there's no ice in this whiskey,' said one of the men.

'I'll run up to the deck and get you some,' said another man, laughing. 'They say the iceberg left a few calling cards.'

So that's what's happened, Kitty thought. I didn't dream that bump, after all; it was an iceberg striking the ship. I wonder how much damage it did.

'It's half past twelve, my lady,' she said, as she re-joined the little group on the promenade deck.

Tabitha looked positively green with the cold.

'Women and children to the boat deck,' one of the officers called into a large megaphone.

'What's the matter, Officer?' asked one of the ladies. 'Is there anything wrong?'

Kitty was amazed at how unconcerned the lady's voice was. Her own heart was beginning to beat rapidly, and her hands felt cold with sweat.

'No, nothing wrong, Madam,' replied the officer. 'We're just taking all possible precautions, that's all. Now, ladies, everyone up to the boat deck, please,' he called, putting the megaphone to his lips again.

'I want to go back to the cabin,' repeated Tabitha. 'I'm cold.'

'Not now, dear,' said Lady Victoria again. She shepherded the two children in front of her towards the lifts, and Kitty followed obediently behind.

By the entrance to the lifts was an elderly lady, her white hair streaming down her back. She was dressed only in a nightdress and wrapper, and she looked distraught with fear.

'Oh, dear, Mrs Irwin,' said Lady Victoria compassionately. 'You will catch a bad chill like that. The boat deck is icy. Shouldn't you go back and dress?'

The woman shook her head. Her teeth were chattering, whether from fear or from cold, Kitty did not know.

'Kitty,' said Lady Victoria, 'would you be kind enough to go down to Mrs Irwin's cabin? It's the one just next to mine. Fetch her fur coat. If we have gone up by the time you get back, we will wait for you just by the entrance to the lift on the boat deck.'

Kitty nodded and ran back downstairs. Mrs Irwin's cabin was in darkness, and it had already begun to cool down; Mrs Irwin had apparently thought of turning off the lights and the heaters, but not of dressing herself. Aren't people queer? thought Kitty.

She rummaged in the wardrobe. Mrs Irwin proved to have two fur coats, and Kitty wasted precious moments in trying to decide which of them would be the warmest and the most suitable — she did not want to be sent back again. Finally she decided on the older of the two. Mrs Irwin might not like to risk the brand-new one in a grubby lifeboat.

Kitty was at the door when she remembered that Mrs Irwin had not got a life-jacket, either. She ran back and reached up to the top of the wardrobe — yes, there was the life-jacket. She bundled it under her other arm and set off, running down the corridor.

There was no sign of the lift. Kitty pressed the button; nothing happened. I'll be quicker on the stairs, she thought. She began to run up the stairs to the boat deck, doing her best not to trip on the bulky fur coat.

Lady Victoria was by the entrance to the lift, Kitty was relieved to see. She was talking to one of the officers. He seemed to be calling out some order — something about 'women and children only' — and Kitty saw that the lifeboat was being lowered on its crane to just beside the boat deck.

'No woman can get onto that,' called one of the men. 'It's too far from the edge of the deck.'

'All women and children down to the promenade deck,' bellowed the officer.

Kitty was almost knocked over by the rush for the

stairs. The passengers were no longer simply bewildered and uneasy; fear was beginning to spread among them.

Suddenly there was a blinding flash, and a rocket rose like a magnificent trail of stars, up into the night sky. Kitty's eyes followed it, her heart cold with fear. That's a distress signal, she thought. The *Titanic* really is in danger.

She hastily looked across to make sure that she could still see Lady Victoria. There were a lot of people in the way, but when they started to move down the steps to the promenade deck, Kitty caught sight of Lady Victoria again — she stood out among the crowd because she was so tall. But she still could not see the children.

They must be behind her, Kitty thought, trying to control her panic. But even when she managed to struggle through the crowd to Lady Victoria's side, there was no sign of Tabitha and Robert. They had both disappeared.

CHAPTER ELEVEN

'*B*ut they were with me only a minute ago!' said Lady Victoria shakily. 'They were beside me. I just turned to say something to Mrs Irwin, and then you arrived and they were gone. Where can they be?'

'They must have gone back to the cabin,' said Kitty, trying to sound more confident than she felt. 'You know what Miss Tabitha is like when she gets an idea in her head. I'll just go down and see. It will only take me a moment. Will you wait here, your ladyship? Maybe they've only gone around the deck to look at the other boats, and then they'll be back in a minute. They've been waiting here for half an hour, after all, and that's a long time for children; they don't like staying still for so long.'

I won't bother with the lift, Kitty thought, as she skidded down the stairs, almost bumping into Captain Smith and Mr Andrews. She flung open the door of the children's cabin and looked in. It was warm and brightly lit, and cosy-looking, but there was no sign of Tabitha and Robert. Kitty dashed across the room and opened the bathroom door — nothing. No sign of them in Lady Victoria's cabin, either. Kitty flew up the stairs again, pushing open the heavy swing doors, out onto the boat deck, into the tingling cold of the frosty air.

The lifeboat was being lowered jerkily to the promenade deck, and there was no one left on the boat deck. Kitty turned and ran back down the steps, to the enclosed part of the promenade deck. The seamen had lashed a few wooden deck-chairs together to make a sort of gangplank, so that the women could climb through a window, along the chairs and into the lifeboat. Most of them seemed very reluctant to do so. It's amazing, thought Kitty: no one seems to have any fear of anything happening to the ship. They're more worried about their dresses than about their lives.

Most of the women had been coaxed into the lifeboat, but Lady Victoria still stood on the deck, head and shoulders above most of the people, anxiously scanning the crowd.

'They're not there, my lady,' called Kitty.

'Oh dear, oh dear — where can they be? Steward — I say, steward! Have you seen my nephew and niece?'

The steward paused in his work of helping the ladies onto the improvised gangplank and turned a blank face to her.

'I've seen the little blond boy, Lady Victoria,' said one of the officers. 'He was up by the Marconi room. I saw him standing at the door, watching the Marconi wireless operator sending out the signals. I told him to go back down to you.'

'Oh, those bad children!' Lady Victoria was obviously relieved. 'Kitty, will you fetch them back, please?'

Kitty started to run up the stairs again. When she was nearly at the top, the officer overtook her.

'There's a lifeboat leaving from the port side, just beside the Marconi room,' he said. 'Get those children into it straight away. I'll tell Lady Victoria what you've done.'

He lowered his voice and whispered in Kitty's ear: 'There aren't enough boats for everybody. The third-class passengers are already panicking. Get those children off as soon as you can.'

Kitty looked at his white, tense face and felt her breath catch in her throat. In that moment she knew, with a cold certainty, that the unsinkable *Titanic* was sinking.

Her heart thudding, Kitty raced along the deck towards the Marconi room. There was, indeed, another lifeboat being loaded up just beside the office. Inside the tiny room, one radio operator was tapping out a signal; another watched him, fidgeting nervously.

'Have you seen a little girl and boy?' Kitty asked breathlessly, hating to interrupt them, but made bold by her terrible anxiety.

One man shook his head absently, his whole attention concentrated on the box in front of him. The other man looked around.

'They were here about ten minutes ago,' he said. 'I told them to go and find their mother.'

Their mother! thought Kitty. That will upset Tabitha even more .... She checked the people on the lifeboat, and the patient queue on the deck: not a sign of a little boy or girl. She clattered halfway down the stairs to the promenade deck, and then stopped. There was no point in going any further. She could see Lady Victoria still standing on the deck, looking anxiously around over the heads of the other women.

Kitty turned and went back up to the boat deck. The ship had begun to lean over to port, and it was definitely dipping more and more to the front, to the bows. How much longer could it stay afloat?

Once again Kitty scanned the people in the life-boat. Everyone who had been waiting was on board; the boat was jerking, and Kitty could see that they were about to lower it.

'Get in, young lady,' shouted an officer. 'There's plenty of room.'

There certainly is, thought Kitty. It looks more than half empty.

'I'm looking for two children,' she explained.

She looked at the boat again, and remembered what the other officer had said about the shortage of lifeboats.

'Why is it going half empty like that?' she asked, too angry to be shy.

'Oh, we're filling up from the hold,' said the officer. 'I sent some men down there to organise it.'

The hold! thought Kitty. That's probably it! Robert would love to see the hold, and Tabitha was desperate to get in out of the cold. They must have followed the men down there. Anyway, if I take the lift, it will only take me a few minutes to check.

She ran across the deck, jumped into the lift and pressed the button. The lift moved down. Through the elaborately ornamented wrought-iron door, Kitty could see the deserted corridors — the carpeted floors, the carved wooden panels, all the lights blazing .... Down to the next floor, and then the next .... I must be near the swimming pool, thought Kitty.

In that same instant, she saw something which made her gasp with horror. Quick as lightning, she pressed the 'up' button, and the lift went shooting back upwards. She had no hope of finding Tabitha and Robert down there. The upper deck was under ten feet of water; the hold must be completely flooded.

The lift moved smoothly through the floors. What if it stops? thought Kitty. What if I get trapped? From now on, I'll trust to the stairs. Quickly she pressed the button marked 'Promenade Deck', and hurried out of the lift the instant that the doors slid open.

The boat had gone. Kitty could hear the creaking as it was lowered towards the sea.

'Did Lady Victoria Fitzgerald go on the boat?' she asked an officer.

He looked at her irritably. 'Who's Lady Victoria Fitzgerald?' he said in a strong Scottish accent. 'Don't bother me, girl. Queue up over there for the next boat.'

Ignoring him, Kitty flew over to a steward.

'Did Lady Victoria go on the last boat?' she asked.

The steward, whose job it was to know all the rich passengers, nodded. 'Yes,' he said. 'She was on it.'

Kitty was conscious of a feeling of relief. She didn't have to worry about anyone else any more; she could just save herself.

'Did she have the children with her?' she asked, just to be sure.

The steward shook his head. 'No,' he said. For a moment, Kitty thought she must be hearing him wrongly. Surely Lady Victoria would never have left without Tabitha and Robert! 'No, she didn't. One of the officers told her they'd gone with you, on the boat from the port side of the boat deck.'

This is worse than any nightmare I've ever had, thought Kitty, running back up the steps to the boat deck in the vain hope that the children might be there after all. There were plenty of people there now, including some children. One was a little girl with a doll in her arms, and Kitty's heart gave a jump of hope; but it was not Tabitha. Although the doll was a little like Princess Mary, this child was younger, and there was no boy with her.

Suddenly Kitty stopped running and stood still. An icy feeling came over her. I know where she's gone, she thought. She's gone to my cabin for her doll. She probably heard something at the Marconi room about the ship sinking, and she would be determined to save the doll.

What's the quickest and safest way to go? wondered Kitty. The deck was slanting sharply; going towards the back of the ship was like walking uphill. How much time do we have? she thought desperately. She struggled along to the end of the boat deck only to find that the gate leading down to the poop deck was closed and locked. In front of it was an officer with a pistol in his hand, and behind the gate was a shouting crowd of third-class passengers.

A rush of anger came over Kitty, almost choking her with its intensity. Not long before, she had seen the first-class passengers being carefully shepherded into the lifeboats; now, on the very same ship, the poorer passengers were being locked away from the boats and safety. 'Let them out!' Kitty screamed, but her voice was lost amidst the passengers' cries.

I must find Tabitha and Robert, Kitty reminded herself. How can I get to my cabin? That officer will never let me through; if he opens the gate, everyone will rush out.

She stood still for a moment, biting her nails in her anxiety. Then an idea came to her. The smoking-room, she thought. I'll go down through the smoking-room. There's a way through there — John showed me.

As she ran she thought of John. His cabin was in the front of the ship, in the doomed bow, which was already slipping under the water. What's happened to him? thought Kitty, in agony. And what's happened to Mrs Healy, and Joan, and Maureen?

Through the smoking-room she ran, startled to see Mr Andrews calmly leaning on the mantelpiece, smoking a cigar. Was it possible that he didn't realise what was happening? He looked up as Kitty dashed through the room, and raised his eyebrows coolly.

'The ship is sinking!' she cried. 'Go to the lifeboats!'

Out of the other door of the smoking-room — no, that was locked too. Kitty hesitated for a moment. Perhaps the steward was wrong; perhaps the children had gone with Lady Victoria, perhaps even now they were safe on the lifeboat — Tabitha grumbling about the cold, Robert wide-eyed with interest in it all ....

But the thought of the two little faces drove Kitty on, back out of the smoking-room. She knew, really, that they were not on that lifeboat. The moment she had seen the doll in the child's arms, she had known where they had gone. Tabitha's doll was immensely important to her; it had almost taken the place of her dead mother. She would never have left it to sink.

Kitty stood at the top of the stairs outside the smoking-room and tried to think. There were crowds of people above her, all struggling to get to the boat deck while there were still a few lifeboats left, but there was no one below her. No one thought of going down when a ship was sinking; everyone went up.

Kitty shut her eyes, trying to picture the ship. She had helped Robert to draw his map, and she could visualise it clearly. Yes: if she went down to the bottom of this staircase, through the cargo hold and up the other staircase, she would be right by her cabin.

The cargo hold was empty of people; there were only piles of boxes and cases and bales, all sliding rapidly down towards the front of the ship. Kitty had a narrow escape from some of the heavy bales, which came rolling rapidly towards her. The ship must be sinking fast, she thought in terror. We haven't got long. At least she was going towards the stern of the boat, and that had seemed to be getting higher and higher out of the water, when she had last looked.

When she reached the opposite door of the cargo hold, there was no one there. She could easily go up the stairs to her cabin.

'Good thinking, clever girl,' she said aloud, encouragingly, to herself. It was something her father used to say to her.

Then she remembered Mike's words: 'He was as brave as a lion, was Patrick. He was the most adventurous of the lot of us.'

'I'm like him,' Kitty had said, in reply.

'You'd be proud of me now, Dad,' she said aloud. Confidently, she raced up the stairs and wrenched open the door of her cabin.

There was no one there. Kitty ran across to her bed, pulled out her box from under it, threw it open and looked in.

Princess Mary lay there, her velvet dress covering her kidskin toes, her blue eyes, magnificently unconcerned, gazing up at Kitty. Tabitha and Robert had not come to the cabin.

CHAPTER TWELVE

$\mathcal{F}$or a moment, Kitty felt sick and dizzy with disappointment. She had been so sure they would be there! She wanted to sit down on her bed and just give up. Her legs ached from running up and down stairs for the past hour, and she suddenly felt completely exhausted. For a moment she leaned against the wall, her eyes closed.

Then she shook herself. I'm sure I'm right, she thought. They'll be somewhere nearby; they may have got lost in this maze of corridors and cabins.

Out of the cabin she went, not bothering to close the door behind her. Up the stairs, her feet ringing on the iron treads. She could hear shouts and cries and wailing from the poop deck.

There was another sound as well, though, nearer to her. Kitty stopped. It was the sound of heartbroken sobs, and it was coming from the cabin next to the steps — the cabin directly above Kitty's own. She listened.

I know those sobs, she thought. I've heard them before, at Corofin House.

'Tabitha?' she yelled, as loudly as she could. She ran to the cabin and rattled the handle, but the door wouldn't open.

And then Robert's voice called: 'Let us out! We're locked in here!'

'Robert! Tabitha!' shouted Kitty, trying desperately to open the door.

'Kitty!' they both screamed from within.

The door must be jammed, thought Kitty. No one would deliberately lock in two children. It must have jammed when the ship tilted. She looked wildly around for someone who might be able to help.

At that moment, the ship gave a convulsive shudder. The floor tilted even more sharply up towards the stern of the ship. Suddenly the cabin door burst open, and out tumbled the two children, their faces white and tear-stained.

'Quick,' said Kitty, taking a hand of each. There was no time for explanations, no time for reassurance. She had to get the children safely into a lifeboat.

They burst out onto the poop deck. There was a huge crowd of people jamming the way to the boat deck. Oh, no! thought Kitty. The gate must still be locked! People were screaming, begging, beating their hands against the bars of the gate; but Kitty fought her way through, dragging the two children behind her.

'Let me through!' she screamed. 'Let me through! I've two children here. Their aunt is up in first class. Let us out!'

'There are two children here,' shouted one of the men to the officer by the gate. 'They're from first class. Perhaps you'll open the gate now. We have our own women and children here, as well, but I don't suppose you care about that!'

I don't care about anything except saving Tabitha and Robert, thought Kitty. Desperately she struggled to the front of the queue, mercilessly dragging the children behind her. Her grip on their wrists was like iron. I'll never let go of them until they're safe, she thought.

She came face to face with the officer at the gate. He was taking a key out of his pocket — slowly, so slowly .... His eyes were on the boat deck above. There was a clanking, then a creak, and then a lifeboat went shuddering and jolting on its journey down the side of the ship towards the flat sea below.

'I'm afraid that's the last boat,' the officer said, as he unlocked the gate.

A great roar of rage and disappointment, anger and terror burst from hundreds of throats. The ship lurched again. The poop deck sloped up behind them like the steep side of a mountain. Several men ran to the railings and dived; others took the time to throw out some of the wooden deck-chairs and cork life-belts before they, too, dived into the freezing water.

Kitty clutched Tabitha and Robert. They had become like her own children; all she could think about was how to save them. She had no fear for herself. The ship was sinking fast, she knew that. The bows were going deeper and deeper into the water. They had very little time.

She looked behind her, at the poop deck, and remembered the two Marconi operators, frantically sending out messages. Surely some other ship would come to rescue them! If only she could keep the children safe until that help arrived ....

'Let's go up to the poop deck,' she said, trying to keep her voice as calm as possible.

Everyone else seemed to have had the same idea, so it was quite a struggle to get up the steps, but at last they reached the poop deck.

'Hold on to this rope thing,' said Kitty urgently, catching hold of a small iron pillar wound about with rope. The angle of the deck was so steep that it felt as if they were about to tumble down into the sea.

'Not a rope thing, Kitty, a capstan,' said Robert, beginning to get back some of his old spirit.

'I'm slipping!' cried Tabitha.

'Hold on tight,' said Kitty encouragingly. 'Look, I'll tell you what I'll do — I'll wind the rope around your waists, so you can't slip back too far. Hold on tightly, though, while I'm doing it.'

Once the rope was safely around the children, Kitty drew a breath of relief. It wasn't much, but it was something. At least now the children couldn't slide down into the water.

She looked around. The sky was full of stars. Even in the quiet darkness of the fields around Drumshee, Kitty had never seen such a magnificently starry night. She wished that she could just stand there quietly, looking at the sky, but she could not shut her ears to the terrible sounds, the shrieks and howls from the other people on the poop deck. Some of them had gathered around a priest, and they were praying. 'Hail Mary, full of grace ...' The prayer rose towards the stars like a desperate final appeal for mercy.

The ship lurched again, and Tabitha screamed. 'The rope is cutting me in two, Kitty!'

Kitty looked down. The poop deck will be underwater in a few minutes, she thought. She looked out to sea: the sixteen lifeboats were floating in the water, and most of them had lanterns, but she could see no sign of any ship coming to the rescue. Both children had begun to cry, and their terrified sobs wrenched at Kitty's heart.

It seems like years since we were up here last, Kitty thought; since that day when Robert jumped on that life-jacket box and blew his whistle .... The life-jacket box had been thrown open now, and it was half empty. As Kitty looked at it, an idea came to her, and with it a little warm spurt of hope.

If she could get the children inside the box, then, at the very least, she could shelter them from the horror of watching the scenes of terror around them. At best .... She could hardly allow herself to think of the best; but the box seemed to be very solidly made, and there were still many life-jackets inside it, each one filled with cork .... Was there any chance that the box might float once the ship sank?

'Robert and Tabitha, listen to me,' Kitty said. To her own amazement, her voice was clear and firm and full of confidence. 'We're going to crawl up the deck and get into that life-jacket box. It will be like a little boat, just for the three of us. Now, keep the rope around your waists; I'm going to lift a few coils of it off the capstan, so you can move. Then we'll have to start crawling. Once I tell you to go, just keep going. Don't look back. And don't give up, whatever you do.'

Robert set off as soon as Kitty gave the word. Agile as a little monkey, he swarmed up the sharply angled deck. Tabitha followed behind; she hesitated once or twice, but Kitty poked her sharply and she went on again. At least she's stopped that terrible sobbing, thought Kitty. Even if this doesn't work, it'll give them something to do — some hope before ....

Even in her own mind, she dared not finish her

sentence. She concentrated on crawling up the sloping deck, inch by painful inch. Once Robert, trying to make progress too quickly, slipped and came crashing down on Tabitha. Kitty grabbed him by his life-jacket and hung on desperately until he regained his balance, and then they were off again.

I won't look up until I've counted to twenty, thought Kitty. That way the journey won't seem too long. She counted up to twenty, counting steadily aloud in an effort to blot out the cries of terror all around her, and then looked up. They were quite close to the box.

Again she started counting, and this time she heard Tabitha and Robert joining in with her.

'... Eighteen, nineteen, twenty.' Kitty looked up. They were beside the box.

Now came the difficult bit. Holding tightly to the edge of the life-jacket box, Kitty pulled herself to her feet, grabbed Robert's arm and hooked it over the side of the box.

'Hold on with all your strength, Robert,' she commanded. She pulled Tabitha up, unwound the rope from her waist and bundled her into the box. Robert watched calmly.

'Now you, you brave boy,' Kitty said lovingly. In a minute, he was freed from the rope and in the box beside his sister.

The ship gave a terrible lurch. For a moment it seemed to stand on its head. Kitty's hand slipped. She clutched desperately at the edge of the box, and felt her feet slide from under her. She felt as if her arm was being torn from her body.

'Saint Brigid, save me!' she screamed.

The whole of the poop deck shuddered, and for a moment Kitty was jerked towards the stern. Quickly she dived, head first, landing in the box on top of Robert and Tabitha.

The poop deck shuddered again and then lurched in the opposite direction, rearing up in the water like a wounded shark. The lid of the life-jacket box flapped over and slammed shut. There were horrendous explosive noises, violent cracking, snapping and roaring. It seemed like the end of the world. Kitty clutched the two children. She knew she was saying something to them, something to calm them, something reassuring, but she could not even hear her own voice; her ears were exploding with the noise.

Suddenly the explosions stopped. Then there was a rending sound, and the solid deck beneath them seem to shift and move. They were lifted into the air and flung from side to side of their box. Then there was a splash, and then silence.

CHAPTER THIRTEEN

The silence seemed extraordinary. Kitty could feel the children moving. Robert said in a trembling voice: 'Are we all right, Kitty?'

'We're all right,' she assured him, in a voice which trembled as much as his own.

'It was Saint Brigid saved us,' said Tabitha. 'I heard you say a prayer to her, just like we did on that day at Drumshee.'

It's funny, thought Kitty: Tabitha, who's always crying about something or other, sounds quite calm. She found the children's hands and clutched them. They both felt quite warm.

'That's right, pet, I did,' she said. 'And Saint Brigid did save us.'

'Are we floating, Kitty?' enquired Robert, his voice steadying.

'It feels like that,' said Kitty. 'Isn't it exciting!' she added, in a voice which she strove to keep calm.

'Can you open the lid, Kitty?' asked Robert.

'No, I think we'd better not, Robert. Not for the moment, anyway,' she said decisively.

'Kitty?' said Tabitha, in a small voice. 'If the ship sank, then Princess Mary drowned, didn't she?'

'I don't know, darling,' said Kitty gently. 'But we're all safe. That's the most important thing.' She tried not to imagine the doll slowly sinking to the sea bed, her blue eyes staring into the darkness of the ocean, the water rippling her golden hair; tried not to think about the possibility that they themselves might soon be sinking the same way.

Tabitha said nothing. In the darkness, Kitty could not tell whether she was crying. But then, to her astonishment, Tabitha said calmly, almost happily: 'I think Princess Mary is in heaven with my Mama.'

'I'm sure she is,' said Kitty thankfully.

Outside, through the planking of the box, Kitty could still hear cries and shouts for help. The box was like a small, dark cocoon. Kitty strove to think of something to say which would keep the children happy and interested, and distract them from the horrors going on in the sea outside.

'It's a pity I didn't know what we were going to do,' she said. 'I could have made some sails for the boat, and then we could have sailed along to America.'

'Just like the Owl and the Pussycat,' said Tabitha happily. 'Do you remember that poem, Robert? Papa used to read it to us, when we were little.'

'Say it for us, Tabitha,' said Kitty. 'I forget it.'

While Tabitha's clear little voice was sending the Owl and the Pussycat to sea in a beautiful pea-green boat, Kitty's mind was working frantically. They were definitely floating, and by some miracle the box seemed to be watertight. She put down her hand and felt the cork-filled life-jackets underneath her. They were quite dry; if any water had come in, it could only be very little. There was probably enough cork in the box to keep it afloat.

Last time I saw the sea, she thought, it was as calm as can be. As long as the wind doesn't rise, we should last for a while in here. It's lovely and warm, what with the three of us and all the life-jackets. The children should be all right as long as they don't panic, and as long as a rescue ship comes soon.

Tabitha had come to the end of her poem. The Owl and the Pussycat were safely married.

'That was lovely,' said Kitty hurriedly. 'Now you say one, Robert.'

While Robert embarked on 'The Grand Old Duke of York', Kitty's thoughts went on working. I wonder whether I should try to raise the lid, she thought, and then decided against it. I'll wait until I can hear a rescue ship, she decided. We'll be much warmer with the lid down. It's a freezing night. In any case, if I try to raise the lid the box might overturn, or the water might come in. She was a little worried about having enough air for them to breathe, but she could see a few sharp lines of starlight along the top of the box, so she knew that there must be some cracks in the lid. We'll sit tight, she thought.

'Now you, Kitty,' said Tabitha.

'Well,' said Kitty, 'I can't remember many poems, but I'll tell you a story. Once upon a time, there were two very good, very brave, very clever children, and they sailed across the Atlantic Ocean in a very little boat ....' It was amazing, Kitty thought, that one part of her mind was working furiously on the problem of how to keep the three of them alive, while all the time she could hear her voice telling this complicated story about pirates and desert islands and a wonderful treasure buried under palm trees.

By the end of the story, the two children were still wide awake, to Kitty's disappointment. After all, it was the middle of the night; she would have expected them to be asleep by now. She was scanning her brain for a boring story to lull them to sleep when suddenly Robert started to sob.

'It's my fault that we got lost,' he said. 'I should have looked in my map. I made a mistake and we went to the wrong cabin ....'

'Oh, don't worry about it.' Tabitha's voice cut in before Kitty had a chance to say anything. 'It's my fault, really. I shouldn't have taken you. You're only little. I should have been looking after you.'

Tabitha's growing up, thought Kitty. She might turn out to be a lovely child in the end.

Aloud, she said: 'Let's count up to a million and then the rescue ship will be here.'

That was a good idea, she thought. The two voices got sleepier and sleepier. By the time they reached one hundred and ten, Robert's voice had dropped out; soon Tabitha's voice trailed away as well. It's even making me sleepy, thought Kitty. She put her head down on her knees, just for a minute ....

When she woke, she thought she must be having a nightmare about being on the boat deck of the *Titanic*. Once again she could hear the officer's voice bawling into a megaphone. She closed her eyes and tried to shut out the sound. It was getting fainter, and Kitty almost drifted off to sleep again; but then her hand struck the solid cork of a life-jacket and she lifted her head, startled and fully awake. Who could be calling through the megaphone?

Moving cautiously, Kitty tried to edge nearer to the narrow crack where the lid of the box met the side. She was very much afraid that she might upset the box and tip them all into the icy sea, but the box stayed quite steady, just rocking slightly. Carefully

Kitty inserted the tips of her fingers into the crack and raised the lid a little.

Everything was very quiet. The sea was littered with broken pieces of wood, and with bobbing white objects. To her horror, Kitty realised that the white objects were people — people who had frozen to death in that arctic sea and become just floating lumps of ice.

Of the ship itself there was no sign. The *Titanic* — the unsinkable *Titanic*, the greatest ship ever made — was gone.

But there was no doubt about it: someone was calling into a megaphone — calling and waiting, and then calling again. By the light of the stars, Kitty could just see a lifeboat. It was some distance from them, but she could see the white uniform of the officer who held the megaphone. They had a lantern, as well; its light flashed among the broken shapes floating on the sea.

'Help!' she yelled, but even to herself her voice sounded small and tinny in that immensity of sky and ocean.

'Help!' she called again.

'What's wrong, Kitty?' said Tabitha, in a shaking voice.

'Is it the ship?' asked Robert.

'Not yet,' said Kitty. 'But it's one of the lifeboats.'

The light was shining in their direction. Surely they must be seen!

'Help!' she screamed. 'We're over here!'

The light swept over them — indifferent to their plight, it seemed to Kitty — and then moved to sweep another portion of the sea. The voice through the megaphone sounded again, but less clearly. The officer had turned his back to them.

'Help!' sobbed Kitty, hardly able to believe that they had not heard her. 'Help — oh, please, help!'

'What's the matter, Kitty?' asked Tabitha's frightened little voice.

Kitty dug her nails deep into the palms of her hands, and took a deep breath. She must not allow the children to become frightened or panicky.

'They're just looking on the other side,' she said, her voice surprisingly calm. 'In a minute they'll turn around, and then they'll see us or hear us.'

'Could we lift the lid up?' asked Tabitha, more cheerfully. 'They might think we're just an old box floating around.'

Kitty drew in another deep breath, and smiled. Of course, that was true. The sailors were looking for people, not for floating bits and pieces from the ship.

'You're such a clever girl, Tabitha,' she said fondly. 'And you're quite right. I'll try to lift the lid a little.'

Cautiously, she raised the lid, using her head to lift it and support it. The icy air rushed into the box, and Kitty could hear Tabitha's teeth begin to chatter.

'Help!' she shouted again. The boat did not turn.

'I'll have to get the lid up a bit more. Then when they turn round, I'll wave to them,' Kitty said, trying to sound reassuring.

Inch by inch, she edged the lid up; but when she had raised it about a foot, the box suddenly lurched.

'It's going to tip over, Kitty!' shouted Robert.

He sounds quite excited, thought Kitty. He's so young that it's all a game to him. Tabitha, though, is probably beginning to guess some of the truth ....

114

Carefully and slowly, Kitty lowered the lid until the gap was only a few inches wide. She could still see out, though. Surely her voice would carry to the lifeboat.

'Help!' she screamed again. 'We're over here!'

Her voice cracked on the last word, and she realised that she should spare her voice and wait until they turned in her direction before she called out again.

'Can I come up next to you, Kitty?' asked Robert.

Kitty hesitated. He might unbalance the box. On the other hand, he had a very clear, carrying voice. She had noticed how often people on the ship had turned around to listen to him, even when he was only talking to Tabitha.

'Come very carefully, then,' she said. 'Be ready to stop the minute I tell you. Tabitha, will you stay there and balance the two of us?'

There was no answer from Tabitha, but Kitty could hear Robert crawling cautiously and slowly across the life-jackets on the bottom of the box. He's doing it very sensibly, Kitty thought. Not many seven-year-olds would be as clever as he is. She felt a rush of pride in him.

He was beside her — and he was as warm as toast, she noticed as his hand touched hers.

'Where's the boat?' he asked. 'Oh yes, I see her. She's turning this way! Now, Kitty, I'll count and we'll shout together. Ready? One, two, three —'

'Help!' they both shouted. For a moment Kitty thought that they had been heard. The boat seemed to turn and head in their direction.

'Let's do it again, Robert,' she said breathlessly. 'You shout too, Tabitha. One, two, three —'

'Help! Help! Help!' they all shouted.

But it was no good. The boat was turning back.

Kitty stared at it in despair. Oh, God, she thought, this can't be happening! After everything we've been through to get this far, they can't just abandon us to die here! She felt tears springing to her eyes, and she fought back a sob.

The next moment she thought her ears were exploding, as an ear-splitting blast from Robert's whistle shrilled out beside her.

'Ship ahoy!' shouted Robert. 'Ship ahoy!' And again came the ear-splitting explosion of the whistle.

This time, there was no mistake. Voices shouted back from the lifeboat, and Kitty could see the officer pointing in their direction. The light came sweeping around — rested on them — wavered and moved on — and then came back to rest on them again.

Kitty saw that a piece of the poop deck had come off with the life-jacket box; they were resting on a more secure base than she had thought. Freed from any worries that they might capsize, she frantically threw the lid open and waved her arms, and once again Robert treated them to a blast from his whistle.

'Stay still,' came the voice from the megaphone. 'Stay very still. We've seen you. We're coming across.'

And then came another voice, without a megaphone, but almost as loud — a voice which Kitty knew well.

'Kitty,' shouted John, 'is that you? Have you got the two children with you?'

CHAPTER FOURTEEN

'And then, Aunt Victoria,' said Robert, conscious of his audience — not just Lady Victoria, but most of the ladies from first class — 'then I just blew my whistle as loudly as I possibly could, and —'

'And Miss Tabitha held the box steady from the other side,' put in Kitty.

'Yes,' agreed Robert. 'Tabby balanced my weight. And then the lifeboat came over and rescued us, and John — our chauffeur,' he added kindly to the other ladies, 'was there on the boat, all dripping wet, and he passed us a thin rope and Kitty tied it to the hook on the side of the box, and then they towed us, and we sang songs all the way back.'

Kitty thought that if Robert hadn't been thoroughly spoilt before, this voyage on the rescue ship, the *Carpathia*, would certainly do it. Everyone wanted to hear the story. Tabitha said nothing, so it was left to Robert to be the spokesman. Kitty herself was only the nursemaid; after Lady Victoria and the captain had praised her bravery and her presence of mind, no one showed too much interest in her. But Robert was a different matter. Passengers, Marconi operators, seamen, everyone down to the cabin boys — they all wanted to hear the story. Again and again the *Carpathia*'s decks rang with the noise of the famous whistle, as Robert demonstrated how he had blown it for the lifeboat.

However, Lady Victoria was taking a lot of trouble with Tabitha. Every day she walked around the ship with her, patiently holding the child's hand and doing her best to talk to her. Tabitha, however, remained pale and withdrawn; and Lady Victoria herself was almost equally pale.

'I'll never forgive myself for going off on that boat and leaving you to find the children,' she had said to Kitty. 'The trouble was, I believed the officer who told me you had gone on one of the other boats. I should have made sure. I can never express my gratitude to you, Kitty, dear. If there is ever anything I can do for you in the future, then you can rely on me to do it.'

Kitty, standing by the railings as the *Carpathia* approached New York, was thinking about Lady Victoria's words. Perhaps I should change my mind about emigrating to America in a few years' time, she thought. Perhaps the sensible thing to do would be to set up as a dressmaker in Ireland. With some help from Lady Victoria, I'd soon establish myself ....

Her eyes followed the dark-haired figure who had come up the steps and was joining her at the rail. Kitty smiled to herself. No, she thought, I'll keep to my plan. As soon as my apprenticeship is finished, I'll come back to America.

'That's the Statue of Liberty,' said John, as he joined her. 'In an hour or so, you'll be on American soil, meeting the Barrys. What relation are they to the children?'

'I think Thomas Barry is their mother's brother, but his wife is American. Lady Victoria told me she belongs to the Society of Friends, whatever that is.'

'I think they must be what people call "Quakers",' said John. 'I don't know much about them.'

Whatever the Society of Friends may be, it must be something nice, thought Kitty a few days later. Jane Barry had taken charge of the children as if they were her own, and she treated Kitty as an honoured friend and the most welcome visitor the house could entertain. Tabitha was given a special mothering, Kitty noticed. The sad little girl was being petted and cosseted in a way that seemed to be just what she needed.

There were three Barry children: Abraham was the same age as Robert, Ellen was five, and Janet was only a year old. The moment Tabitha entered the house, she became passionately attached to baby Janet. It was her greatest delight and privilege to help to bathe the baby, to brush the baby's soft brown hair, to play with her, to amuse her, and above all to sit with the baby held securely on her lap.

'Tabitha needs to be loved,' said Jane Barry to Kitty, a week later. 'She needs someone to need her, also, and Janet loves and needs her.'

'Yes, ma'am,' said Kitty, a little uncomfortably. She agreed, but she felt a little awkward: Mrs Barry always said 'Tabitha' and 'Robert' to her, whereas Lady Victoria was always careful to call them 'Miss Tabitha' and 'Master Robert'.

'Don't call me "ma'am",' Mrs Barry said, smiling. 'Call me Jane. We are all equal in the eyes of God.'

This was even more embarrassing. Kitty could just imagine Lady Victoria's horror if she were to hear her nursemaid calling her sister-in-law 'Jane'.

And yet, Lady Victoria was very nice in her own

way. She had had a long talk with Kitty that morning, and Kitty was still thinking about what she had said.

'You see, Kitty,' Lady Victoria had said, 'my mother, who is old and infirm, has heard about the loss of the *Titanic*, and she cannot be persuaded that we are all still alive. She thinks that people are lying to her when they tell her that the children and I escaped. I think I shall have to go home, to reassure her. In any case, I find that I cannot enjoy myself here in New York. I can't forget all those poor people who were drowned that night. More than fifteen hundred of them, Kitty! The horror of it won't leave me.' Lady Victoria stopped speaking and stood looking out of the window, her face white and drawn.

Kitty clenched her hands. She had been trying to avoid thinking about the *Titanic*. Now, suddenly, it all came flooding back. All the people who had danced at the céilí; the white-bearded captain who had been so nice to Robert; Mr Andrews, the designer of the ship, smoking his cigar and calmly awaiting death; the electricians keeping the lights of the ship blazing until the last possible moment; the young Marconi operator desperately sending out his SOS signals .... The images were unbearable, and Kitty could not hold back a sob.

Lady Victoria turned from the window and patted her hand. After a moment she continued: 'Still, that does not mean that you have to return, Kitty. If you wish to stay on for the six months, Mrs Barry will be very happy to have you. I will leave your return ticket with her. It is for you to decide. My mind is made up: I leave for Ireland next Friday. The children are settled and happy; I talked with them both this morning, and they would like to stay with their cousins and their aunt and uncle. Think it over, my dear, and let me know this evening.'

Kitty was still thinking it over while she listened to Mrs Barry — she just could not call her Jane, even in her mind. She looked out at the garden and watched the children. It was a lovely sunny day, and Robert and Abraham were building themselves a tepee under some trees. They were wearing gaily painted feathers in their hair; apart from that, each wore only a piece of brown towelling around his middle.

Kitty smiled as she watched. The night before, Robert had given her a great lecture on the lives and customs of American Indians. He had given up his obsession with boats; Indians were now his main interest in life.

It's good for him to have a boy of his own age to play with, Kitty thought. He's becoming much less spoilt, much less of a show-off. He would always be a happy child, she knew, and he would always go through life in a sunny way.

If only poor little Tabitha had some of his confidence, Kitty thought.

Tabitha was sitting on a bench, rocking baby Janet on her knee. Her face had a serious, intent expression, but she looked peaceful and happy. Kitty muttered a quick excuse to Mrs Barry, then ran down to the garden and sat on the bench beside Tabitha.

'Tabby,' she said affectionately, 'would you be a bit sad if I went back to Ireland with your Aunt Victoria at the end of the week?'

She looked carefully at Tabitha. Tabitha looked

startled, but not too upset. At the moment, thought Kitty, her mind is full of the baby and of her Aunt Jane. This is a good time to go.

'Would you come back to see me?' Tabitha asked, after a moment.

Kitty nodded. 'Yes,' she said. 'You see, Tabby, I'm going to learn to be a dressmaker. Mrs Neylon is going to teach me. Then, when I've learned everything that she knows, I'm going to come back to America and be a dressmaker here.'

'And marry John?' asked Tabitha, in interested tones. 'One of the sailors told Robert that John loves you.'

Kitty laughed and blushed a little, and kissed Tabitha. 'Keep that a secret,' she warned. 'I might do. And I'll tell you what: if I do, you can be my bridesmaid — if your aunt allows you, of course. I'll make you a beautiful dress.'

Tabitha smiled contentedly and busied herself with stroking the baby's hair. Kitty hesitated. She had promised Lady Victoria to ask Tabitha something, and this was the time to do it.

'Miss Tabitha,' she said eventually.

'I like it better when you call me Tabby,' interrupted Tabitha.

'I like it better, too,' confessed Kitty. 'Tabby, your Aunt Victoria would like to buy you a present before she goes.' She faltered a little, looking anxiously at the little face. Tabitha had never mentioned Princess Mary since that terrible night when the *Titanic* had sunk. 'She wondered if you'd like a doll,' Kitty finished.

Tabitha's face did not change.

'No, thank you,' she said politely. 'I prefer babies.'

Kitty smothered a smile. 'I don't think she could

buy you one of those,' she said. Then an idea came to her. 'I'll tell you what,' she said. 'I'll ask her to buy some material, and we'll make the baby a new dress. You can choose the stuff and I'll help you with the sewing.'

'Oh, that would be lovely!' said Tabitha enthusiastically. 'Janet can wear the dress to your wedding.'

Kitty was still smiling about that when she met John that afternoon.

'Well, I'm off to Boston on Friday,' was the first thing he said. Then he asked, 'What are you smiling about?'

'Well, I'm off to Ireland on Friday,' Kitty told him, not liking to mention Tabitha's wedding plans.

John's eyes widened with surprise, but when she finished explaining he nodded in approval.

'The sooner you go, the sooner you'll come back,' he said. 'Now, promise that you'll write. I've written down my sister's address for you. When you come back to America, come straight there. Promise.'

'I promise,' Kitty said, and she knew that she would keep the promise.

CHAPTER FIFTEEN

'So, Granny, you were quite right. It was bad luck to take the necklace away from Drumshee.' Kitty kissed old Annie and smiled at Mike and Maggie.

'I'll keep the necklace while I'm at Drumshee,' she added, 'but if I do go out to America, then it will go to little Bridget. I won't take it away again.'

'You look years older,' said Maggie lovingly. 'There's a great change in you. You're quite the young lady now.'

Kitty smiled. 'I feel as if it's been about a year since I was last at Drumshee,' she said. 'I'll go and see Mrs Neylon tomorrow,' she added. 'Lady Victoria says she'll pay the premium for my apprenticeship, and she won't take no for an answer. I'm really looking forward to starting work and being able to earn my own living.'

'Come and put the ducks in with me,' said Mike, knocking out his pipe on the hob of the big fireplace. 'That'll bring your feet back to earth, if anything can.'

'Do that. I'll have the tea ready by the time you get back,' said Maggie, putting the sleeping baby into old Annie's arms. She began bustling around the kitchen, cutting a slab of butter and taking down a freshly baked cake of soda bread from the old dresser.

The ducks proved easier work than usual. A fox barked, down by the Isle of Maain, and the ducks pushed and jostled their way into their house in record time.

'You go back in, Uncle Mike,' said Kitty. 'I'll follow you in a moment.'

He nodded and turned to go; then, after a moment's hesitation, he turned back and stroked Kitty's hair.

'The courage of you!' he said wonderingly. 'You're the image of Patrick, God bless you.'

After Mike had gone, Kitty stood still for a moment, smiling to herself. She had been putting painful thoughts of her father out of her head for years; but now it was lovely to be here, at Drumshee, surrounded by memories of him.

'It's the first of May tomorrow, and it's going to be a gorgeous day,' she thought, making her way out of the orchard and up towards the old *cathair*. The western sky above the hill opposite was like a stained-glass window, streaked with pink and rose and deep blue.

Kitty stood gazing at it for a moment. Then she turned and pushed her way under the old ash tree. She knelt down on the ground beside the little shrine, and looked at the strangely carved stone figure.

'Thank you, Saint Brigid,' she whispered. 'Thank you for bringing me safely back to Drumshee.'